How to Be a High Performance Believer In Low Octane Days

How to Be a High Performance Believer In Low Octane Days

By Dick Mills and Dave Williams

Unless otherwise indicated, all Scripture quotations are taken from the King James Version of the Bible.

HOW TO BE A HIGH PERFORMANCE BELIEVER IN LOW OCTANE DAYS

First Printing 1996

ISBN 0-938020-46-3

Published by Decapolis Publishing
PO BOX 80386
Lansing, Michigan 48908
(517) 321-2780 or (517) 321-CARE

ORDER LINE (800) 888-7284

Books by Dick Mills

He Spoke, and I Was Strengthened
How To Have A Happy Marriage
The Spirit-filled Believer's Daily Devotional
The Spirit-filled Life Bible, Editor
— World Wealth Section
The Spirit-filled Believer's Topical Bible
The Messiah and His Hebrew Alphabet
The Four Loves
A New Wave of the Holy Spirit

Write for more materials:

Dick & Betty Mills Ministries
PO Box 2600
Orange, California 92669

Books by Dave Williams

AIDS Plague
Beauty of Holiness
Christian Job Hunter's Handbook
Desires of Your Heart
Depression, Cave of Torment
Finding Your Ministry & Gifts
Genuine Prosperity
Getting To Know Your Heavenly Father
Grand Finale Revival
Growing Up in Our Father's Family
Laying On of Hands
Lonely in the Midst of a Crowd
The New Life...The Start of Something Wonderful
La Nueva Vida (The New Life...SPANISH)
Pacesetting Leadership
The Pastor's Pay
Patient Determination
Revival Power of Music
Remedy for Worry and Tension
Secret of Power With God
Seven Signposts on the Road to Spiritual Maturity
Slain in the Spirit — Real or Fake?
Somebody Out There Needs You
Success Principles From the Lips of Jesus
Supernatural Soulwinning
Thirty-Six Minutes with the Pastor
Tongues and Interpretation
Understanding Spiritual Gifts

Write for a current catalog of faith-building materials:

Mount Hope Books
A Division of Decapolis Publishing House
202 S. Creyts Rd. Lansing MI 48917
Tel: (517) 321-2780 or (517) 321-CARE
ORDERLINE: (800) 888-7284

Special Thanks

We would like to give special thanks to our editorial staff and team: Linda Teagan, Heather Gleason, Dawn Goodman, Tonya Clark, Jeanne Mills, Glenda Rozeboom, and Eldon Langworthy. Thanks for all your hours of assistance and hard work in seeing this project through to completion.

Contents

Contents (Continued)

Contents (Continued)

Chapter One

WHAT HIGH PERFORMANCE LIVING CAN DO FOR YOU

by Dave Williams

How would you like to become a hundred to a thousand times more productive? You can, and you won't be expending much more energy than you are right now. You can do it through high performance living! High performance living pays off in many ways. First, high performance believers are survivors and thrivers. As you study the New Testament, you find that only those believers who activate the high performance disciplines will be able to stand against the end-time onslaughts of the enemy. The warfare will become too intense for those who choose to chug-chug along.

Second, high performance believers are achievers. You will never see someone driving a low performance race car in a high performance race. They know that if they tried it, they would end up ashamed and embarrassed at the results...or lack of results. It's the high performance entries that win. And remember, St. Paul said, "Run in such a way as to get the prize." In other words, "Race to win!"

Third, high performance believers have great joy. Have you ever noticed the exuberant joy a winner exhibits after a victory? There is something about being a winner that creates a bubbly joy that everyone notices. Joyless, sadsack believers are that way because of one of two reasons: either they haven't obeyed God in some area, or they haven't put the right additives in their spiritual engines. High performance believers have poured in the correct spiritual additives and, as a result, move with tireless energy and strength. "The joy of the Lord is your strength," (Nehemiah 8:10).

Fourth, high performance believers have an unusual beauty. There is something appealing about them. You may not be able to pin point what makes them attractive, yet you know something special is there. They are beautiful. They may not have a striking physical appearance, but there is a radiance about them. When St. Peter listed the ingredients for high performance living in his second epistle, he painted an amazing word picture. Each additive is like a precious jewel — strung together to make an invisible necklace. When a high performance believer puts on this "spiritual necklace", it brings an unseen yet noticeable beauty to them.

What about you? Are you living a high performance Christian life? Or are you barely making it, limping through life with a gummed up spiritual engine? Are you ready to put some high performance additives into your spiritual engine? Then get ready for an exciting adventure into high performance living. Dick and I will give you, from God's Word, nine spiritual additives that will soup up your performance and cause you to run easily in the fast lane of life. Once you've added them, you'll have what it takes to survive any enemy threat: you'll achieve more than you ever dreamed; you'll experience a new joy bursting in your soul giving you inexhaustible energy and strength; and you'll be the attractive believer God called you to be.

Are you ready for an adventure? Are you ready to receive the additives that will make your life one of higher performance than you've known in the past? Then let's get started!

Chapter Two

RACING, OR RUNNING ON EMPTY?

By Dick Mills & Dave Williams

You and I are in a race. Paul said it.

"Do you not know that in a race all the runners run, but only one gets the prize? Run in such a way as to get the prize. Everyone who competes in the games goes into strict training. They do it to get a crown that will not last; but we do it to get a crown that will last forever. Therefore I do not run like a man running aimlessly; I do not fight like a man beating the air. No, I beat my body and make it my slave so that after I have preached to oth-

ers, I myself will not be disqualified
for the prize."

(1 Corinthians 9:24-27 NIV)

Why is it so many who profess to know Jesus Christ
are struggling? Instead of victory, they experience defeat.
Instead of joy, they experience exhaustion. They feel they
won't even be able to finish the race, much less win it!
Like the refrain from a popular song, they feel they are
"running on empty."

The secret to experiencing the full strength and joy of
loving Jesus is the subject of this book. Success in any en-
deavor takes preparation and work. However, we must prepare and work in the right way. In 2 Peter 1:5-7, we are
shown nine specific spiritual qualities that will assure that
we are running like high performance race cars with high
octane fuel and not sputtering along like rusted out clunk-
ers with no gas in the tank.

Think for a moment. If you were competing in an automobile race which offered a huge reward to the winner, and
you could choose the race car you would drive, would you
pick:

■ A no performance car?

■ A low performance car?

■ A mediocre performance car?

■ A high performance car?

Of course you would say, "I want the high performance car." It only makes sense, when so much is at stake, to want the very best. You would also make sure that you had the very best fuel, the best pit crew, the best tires, the best of everything to assure that you came in first. Before the race, you would train your body and reflexes to be at their strongest, so you could withstand the physical stresses of race day. And when the starting gun went off, you wouldn't meander aimlessly from one side of the track to the other, you would race with purpose and speed, as fast as you could, to the finish line.

Why is it then, that so many who profess to know Christ are content to live no performance, low performance, or mediocre performance lives when there is immeasurably more at stake than just money? We are in a race for eternity. The precious lost of this world are depending on high performance believers to rescue them from a fiery eternity. They are counting on us to be the very best Christians we can be.

The Bible describes three sets of spiritual dynamics in a successful Christian life. Each of the three sets are distinctly characterized by the action of the Holy Spirit in our lives. They are:

■ 1. The nine-fold *Fruit of the Spirit* is vital to Christian growth, development, and character building, and is described in Galatians 5:22-23.

■ 2. The nine *Gifts of the Spirit* are vital to missionary-evangelism and church growth. These are itemized in 1 Corinthians 12:8-10.

■ 3. The nine *Graces of the Spirit* are qualities that enhance the life and testimony of the Christian believer. In this book, we call them "Nine Additives for High Performance Living," and they can be found in 2 Peter 1:5-7.

The New King James translation specifies these nine spiritual qualities as:

■ 1. Diligence — The motivating word.

■ 2. Faith — The set in motion word.

■ 3. Virtue — The active internal excellence word.

■ 4. Knowledge — The having the facts word.

■ 5. Self-Control — The keeping your cool word.

■ 6. Perseverance — The persevering word.

■ 7. Godliness — The heavenly minded word, coupled with "down to earth" practicality.

■ 8. Brotherly-Kindness — The caring for the brotherhood word.

■ 9. Love — The "I only want what is best for you" word.

By internalizing these nine qualities, you will find that your Christian walk is filled with strength, purpose, and direction. You will find that nurturing these traits in your life will grant you a feeling of well-being and success. You will race, not run on empty!

"That which is already present must be strengthened. The work begun in the heart must be carried on to completion. All these graces must abound more and more."
                    —William Hendricksen

Chapter Three

THE WORD "ADD" – EPICHOREGEO

By Dick Mills

Although "add" is not one of the nine additives, it is the word that gives cohesion to the other graces and virtues.

"Add" in the Greek New Testament is EPICHOREGEO (epp-ee-khor-ayg-eh-oh) and appears five times in a serving, ministering mode. EPICHOREGEO has a very colorful background tracing back to "choros" the round-dance. Then "chorous" the choir or the dancers. Next "choregeo" the choir leader or the dance leader. After "choregeo," the word then progressed to mean the benefactor who defrayed all the costs, or the one who was the underwriter for the total production. Adding the prefix "epi" to "choregeo" according to the Pulpit Commentary, "indicates profusion in the supply." Expositor's Greek New Testament states, "as men took pride in the lavish fulfillment of supplying members of the chorus, the word came to denote liberal supply."

EPICHOREGEO (add) in 2 Peter 1:5 encourages us to supplement our faith with all the graces and virtues that are named. "Epi" adds the dynamic of intensity to our action so that we are acting without reticence, caution or restraint. "Add" can be likened to a baker stirring a cake mix with select, chosen ingredients that enrich the texture and enhance the flavor. Therefore, when the writer says, "add to your faith, virtue, etc.," he is urging us to stir into our Christian personality quality ingredients.

"ADD"

TRANSLATIONS

Basic English — *Joining supply*

Douay Confraternity — *Minister*

Fenton — *Drill yourselves*

Spencer — *Superadd to your faith*

Cunnington — *In your faith provide*

Wuest — *Provide lavishly*

Knox — *Crowning your faith*

Modern Language — *Supplement your faith*

Moffatt — *Furnish your faith*

New American — *Undergird your faith*

Barclay — *Equip your faith*

Translator's — *Support your faith*

Jordon — *Put into your faith*

"Peter urges his people to equip their lives with every virtue. That equipment must not be simply a necessary minimum, but lavish and generous. The very word, EPICHOREGEO, is an incitement to be content with nothing less than the loveliest and the most splendid Christian life."

—William Barclay

Chapter Four

HOW WILL YOU BE WELCOMED INTO HEAVEN?

By Dave Williams

Have you ever wondered what kind of entrance you'll have into heaven? Will it be a grand, spectacular entrance? Or will it be a humdrum, run-of-the-mill entrance? There are two types of entrances into heaven.

In 2 Peter, Chapter one, we find the nine additives that give us high performance living now, and that also guarantee an entrance into heaven overflowing with pomp and majesty in the future. Peter believed these additives were so important that he said, three times, that he would teach these spiritual truths as long as he lived — he couldn't emphasize them enough. He said,

■ 1. "Even though you already know these things, I'm going to keep teaching them to you over and over again."

■ 2. "As long as I'm alive, I'm going to continue to remind you of these things."

■ 3. "In fact, I'm going to tell you so many times, that even after I leave this life, these things will ring constantly in your heart and mind. You are going to remember them."

What are the additives that Peter felt were so important that he was willing to devote his life to making sure believers understood them? What habit patterns did Peter describe that would determine the type of Christian you would become, and even determine the kind of entrance into heaven you'll experience when this life is over? Let us read what he said:

> "Simon Peter, a servant and an apostle of Jesus Christ, to them that have obtained like precious faith with us through the righteousness of God and our Savior Jesus Christ: Grace and peace be multiplied unto you through the knowledge of God, and of Jesus our Lord, according as His divine power hath given unto us all things that pertain unto life and godliness, through the knowledge of Him that hath called us to glory and virtue: Whereby are given unto us exceeding great and precious promises: that by these ye might be partakers of the divine nature, having escaped the corruption that is in the

*world through lust. And beside this, giving all **diligence**, add to your faith **virtue**; and to virtue **knowledge**; And to knowledge **temperance**; and to temperance **patience**; and to patience **godliness**; And to godliness **brotherly kindness**; and to brotherly kindness **charity**. For if these things be in you, and abound, they make you that ye shall neither be barren nor unfruitful in the knowledge of our Lord Jesus Christ. But he that lacketh these things is blind, and cannot see afar off, and hath forgotten that he was purged from his old sins. Wherefore the rather, brethren, give diligence to make your calling and election sure: for if ye do these things, ye shall never fall: For so an entrance shall be ministered unto you abundantly into the everlasting kingdom of our Lord and Savior Jesus Christ. Wherefore I will not be negligent to put you always in remembrance of these things, though ye know them, and be established in the present truth. Yea, I think it meet, as long as I am in this tabernacle, to stir you up by putting you in remembrance; Knowing that shortly I must put off this my tabernacle, even as our Lord Jesus Christ hath shewed me. More-*

> *over I will endeavor that ye may be*
> *able after my decease to have these*
> *things always in remembrance."*

> *2 Peter 1:1-15*

When the Bible speaks of the "Kingdom of God," it usually refers to everything under the authority of God, both in heaven and on earth. But when the words "everlasting kingdom" appear, as they do in verse 11, it is talking about the heavenly kingdom, or heaven. When a believer dies, his spirit immediately leaves his body and departs to be with the Lord.

> *"Therefore we are always confi-*
> *dent, knowing that, whilst we are at*
> *home in the body, we are absent from*
> *the Lord: (For we walk by faith, not*
> *by sight.) We are confident, I say,*
> *and willing rather to be absent from*
> *the body, and to be present with the*
> *Lord."*

> *2 Corinthians 5:6-8*

When this happens, the believer will experience one of two kinds of entrances into heaven, depending upon whether or not that believer actively made use of the nine spiritual additives Peter lists, which we will discuss in detail later. For now, however, let's simply look at the nine additives to high performance living:

■ 1. Diligence

■ 2. Faith

■ 3. Virtue

■ 4. Knowledge

■ 5. Self-control

■ 6. Perseverance

■ 7. Godliness

■ 8. Brotherly kindness

■ 9. Love

In 2 Peter 1, verse 11 it says, *"For so an entrance shall be ministered unto you* ***abundantly*** *into the everlasting kingdom of our Lord and Savior Jesus Christ."* The word "abundantly" means, "grand, majestic, spectacular, lavish." Peter is talking about the kind of entrance into heaven the victorious, high performance believer will experience; the one who has poured the nine spiritual additives into his "spiritual engine" and has done more than just mark off time while on earth; one who raced with purpose in every step.

Peter, in a nutshell, describes the two types of believers:

■ **1. The High Performance Believer** — This is the one who has added the nine ingredients, escaped corruption, is fruitful, knows his mission, and has purpose and vision. In Peter's words, "he can see far off." Not only does he have vision for today, but he makes decisions based upon tomorrow and eternity.

■ **2. The Defeated Believer** — This is the one who, for some reason or other, has not made use of the nine additives. He constantly stumbles, falls, and is barren. That means he is unfruitful and relatively useless as it relates to any meaningful ministry on earth. He is blind, or has no vision, and as a result, just stumbles through a life of meaningless existence.

When the high performance believer goes to heaven, he will bask in the great celebration of his arrival. In fact, according to verse 11, an abundant entrance will be ministered to him. In other words, residents of heaven, ready to minister, will gather to meet him when he's entering the portals of glory!

In fact, Peter paints a beautiful word picture here. The apostles would frequently use Roman terms, understandable to the people of their day, in order to explain spiritual truths. Paul often used military terms to describe spiritual images. The Christian's armor, for instance, described in Ephesians Chapter six, was an illustrated spiritual truth using the Roman soldier's armor as a tool for understanding the spiritual concept. Peter, likewise, used a Roman custom to help believers understand what he meant by a grand entrance into heaven. Whenever a Roman commander and his legion would return home after conquering lands and winning territory for the Roman Empire, the Emperor would do something wonderful. He would declare a national holiday in honor of the commander's victory. Nobody would work that day. Instead, the citizens would get all dressed up in their finest attire and gather at the city gate.

Great preparations were made for the conquering hero's arrival with his troops. Dancers would be ready to dance. Singers would prepare to sing, and the band tuned up for a great parade marking the arrival of the victors. A lavish banquet was arranged in their honor. Joyful anticipation flooded the entire city.

Finally, when the victorious commander and his troops drew in sight, the trumpets blared a fanfare heard throughout the city, the choirs sang, and the dancers swirled through the streets in joyful abandon. What a welcome it was to the successful warriors as they marched through the city gate to all the excitement. The Emperor would embrace the commander in greeting and place a crown of laurel on his head. Then the Emperor would lavish gifts and rewards upon the commander and his men.

It was a day of rejoicing. A celebration. Afterward, the Emperor would give the commander charge over an entire region of the Empire. What a reward!

Jesus told us about a similar celebration for the high performance believer. He said the productive servants would be given charge over much in the kingdom. But the non-productive, low performance servants would lose even what little they had. The low performance believers are still His servants, but will not get any rewards. They won't rule and reign the way the high performance believers will (Matthew 25:14-28).

The Roman celebration and rewards ceremony is a picture of the high performance believer's entrance into heaven. Can you picture it? There is an announcement throughout all of heaven, "Joe Christian will be arriving at Gate One." Then all of the Holy City prepares for Joe's arrival. Heaven's residents gather at the city gates. Jesus comes to greet Joe. The heavenly choirs begin to sing, and angels dance in great celebration, welcoming Joe to his new home in heaven. What excitement! Then while he is still reeling from all the grandeur of his arrival, Jesus walks over, hugs him and says, "Welcome home, Joe! Thank you for a job well-done." Joe made a spectacular entrance into heaven, and after all the honors and celebration of his homecoming, Jesus gives Joe his millennial assignment of honor. What a day that will be!

But if there is such a thing as a glorious, splendid, spectacular entrance into heaven, there must likewise be another kind of entrance into heaven. There is, indeed, another kind of entrance which Paul talked about as being "Saved, yet so as by fire" (1 Corinthians 3:15). In other words, some will make it into heaven because of their faith in Jesus

Christ; but because they have lived such defeated, low performance lives, their entrance will be without fanfare. Some put it this way: "They made it into heaven, but it was hell getting there!"

Who gets a "saved, yet so as by fire" type of entrance into heaven? It's the defeated believer, the slothful traveler, who is spiritually blind, or at best near-sighted ("cannot see afar off"). It is the believer who only thinks about things of earth, never making decisions in light of eternity, and is only concerned about how he feels or what kind of mood he's in. Let's give him a name. How about "Doby Defeat?"

Doby Defeat will drag up to the heavenly gates, his shoulders bent over from all the burdens he carried on earth and from all the wrong done him by others. Doby always played the victim on earth, never the victor. His problems were always somebody else's fault. But he named Jesus as his Savior, so here he is. Heaven at last!

The heavenly announcer proclaims, "Doby Defeat, arriving at Gate Two, saved, yet so as by fire." Not much celebration occurs. Doby walks through the gate, relieved that his weary journey through life is over. Life was one big frustration for him anyway, full of depressing thoughts and complications. Doby walks up to Jesus and is welcomed to heaven. And though Jesus welcomes him home, he doesn't hear the words, "Well done, thou good and faithful servant." After all, Jesus can't lie. Doby didn't do well, wasn't good, and wasn't faithful. So he missed those encouraging words every believer longs to hear.

Doby remembers some of his "good deeds" so he gathers them up into a box. First the wood goes in, then the hay, and finally the stubble. He bends over to lay his box of good works at the feet of Jesus, and before they even touch the ground, the fire of God's glory burns them to ashes. Even what Doby thought he had is now gone.

Yes, Doby made it into heaven. He made it because he exercised faith in Jesus Christ. Faith in Christ alone is what will carry us into heaven. But how we live on earth will determine our kind of entrance into heaven, our rewards, and our millennial position. Honor and rewards escaped this defeated, low performance believer. He had a foggy vision, lacked purpose and mission, and stumbled around in life because he forgot the things Peter said to remember. He finished so far behind the race that the happy crowds that welcomed the winner home had long since gone.

What are you doing on earth? Is your life more than just checking off meaningless days on the calendar? Every action, every decision, and every measure of time you spend here on earth, has implications which will carry over into eternity. Today you are creating a record for eternity. Why not create a winning record with the nine spiritual additives for high performance living?

Chapter Five
ADDITIVE #1: DILIGENCE — SPOUDE
THE "MOTIVATING" WORD
By Dick Mills

This is a very aggressive word. It is the word to get you ready for adding on, or supplementing the other eight qualitative virtues. This word will motivate you not to quit until all nine additives are functioning in your spiritual walk with the Lord.

SPOUDE (spoo-day) — Strong's #4710, appears 12 times in the New Testament. Our words "speed" and "speedy" come from this word. SPOUDE combines two qualities we all need: speed and skill. SPOUDE can be defined as "fast and nimble," "swiftness and agility." Kittel calls it a "Holy Zeal." Modern definitions are: "to get going, to waste no time, an earnest haste to get on with it, a concentrated pursuit." It combines desire and all out effort. It could be explained as "putting feet on your dreams," "doing something with your hopes," or "activating your giftings." SPOUDE is the opposite of reticence, laziness, procrastination, or superficial frivolity."

By putting diligence (SPOUDE) before all the other virtues, the writer is giving us a basic orientation for what is to follow. SPOUDE makes a person eager to do something beneficial. It implies a readiness to expend energy plus making an all-out effort. Some consulted translators tersely said, "trying hard."

By combining speed and skill, it is easy to see how the word diligence (SPOUDE) blends time and energy — some people can move fast, but they leave a big mess everywhere they go. Human tornados can cover a lot of territory speedily but leave a path of debris behind them. Swift, not smooth, is the word to describe them.

Others are very skillful, but move like a slow freight train. You would think rigor mortis was setting in. Someone has described this crowd as "so slow it would take them an hour and a half to watch a sixty minute television program."

SPOUDE motivates you to be able to expedite all these other virtues and graces with rapid stride and total stress-free concentration. It is fast, active, and intensive productivity. SPOUDE blends both factors into the one component: "Diligence."

"DILIGENCE"

TRANSLATIONS

Fenton — *Use every effort*

New English — *You should try your hardest*

Moffatt — *Continue to make it your whole concern*

Basic English — *Take every care*

Clarence Jordan — *Do your dead level best*

Wuest — *Having added on your part every intense effort*

Wand — *You must be up and doing*

*"The Christian has his own
particular history in relation to his
Lord. He lives between the 'no
longer' and the 'not yet.'"*
                    —Colin Brown

Chapter Six

HABIT PATTERNS

By Dave Williams

What determines whether or not we become high performance believers? What is it that affects the kind of entrance into heaven we will one day experience? In answer to these questions, I have observed one major key factor: OUR HABIT PATTERNS.

A defeated, low performance believer — one who will experience a "saved, yet so as by fire" homecoming — has developed certain habits in life that characterize his existence. These habits can be changed by humility, teachability, and yielding to the Holy Spirit. But the low performance believer is usually too sensitive, irritable, and defensive to learn anything new and fresh. When a concerned Christian offers to help him change his defeatist patterns, the low performance believer will deny that he has a problem. He will shuffle the blame, point out other people's problems to get the focus off his own, and may even slander his helper for trying to help. He hasn't learned that the wounds of a friend are better than the kisses of an enemy. His self-esteem is somewhere in the basement, and it's obvious to everyone but himself.

Let's look at ten of the habit patterns of low performance believers:

■ **1. Procrastination** — They consistently do low-priority work at the expense of high-priority involvement.

■ **2. Slothfulness** — You can see it in the way they walk and hear it in the way they talk.

■ **3. A spiritually lazy existence** — They would rather play than pray. If the church has a feast, they'll be there. If the church calls for a fast, forget it!

■ **4. Judgemental attitude** — Listen to the way they talk about others. They criticize people who are trying to do what's right; they lambaste people who have stumbled in some way.

■ **5. Lack of interest in the Bible** — To them the Bible has become uninteresting and sometimes even repulsive. Yet, quite often they'll spout off their interpretation of certain passages as if God has given them exclusive inside information.

■ **6. No interest in a private prayer time** — Oh, yes, they will religiously bow their heads in a public church service, but when it comes to the "secret closet"...well, there just isn't one.

■ **7. Lack of generosity** — Quite often the low performance believer will look for reasons not to give to benevolent enterprises. "It's their own fault that they are hungry," they declare.

■ **8. No focus on eternity** — Their decisions are exclusively based upon the "here-and-now." They have no real zeal for winning lost souls to Christ.

■ **9. Operate by mood rather than principle** — Their happiness is limited to what kind of mood they're in at the moment. Someone may ask, "Hey, Doby! Do you want to go play some basketball?" "Naw," Doby responds, "I'm not in the mood." Or, "Doby, let's go to the prayer meeting tonight!" "Naw, I don't feel like going," he responds.

■ **10. They view themselves as victims** — Low performance believers will not accept responsibility for their own lives. All their problems are the result of bad luck, other people, or wrong circumstances.

Now, it's easier than you'd think to move from low performance to high performance habit patterns. It starts by recognizing the indicators of low performance living, asking God to forgive and heal, then moving on to high performance living by using the additives God offers. It's simple once you get past the dreadful realization that one or more of these habits have crept in. It's painful when you come to grips with the fact that you're in the pits instead of in the race. But it's not hopeless! If you have found any of the habits of low performance believers lurking in your life, get ready for a miracle! If you'll put in the spiritual additives and get back in the race, God will put you on "fast forward," and your life will take on a whole new aspect of success.

We've talked about the habits of low performance believers. Now let's look at a word all high performance believers understand. This one word describes their way of life. It's the first additive to high performance living. Here it is: Diligence.

Chapter Seven

THE HABIT OF DILIGENCE

By Dave Williams

Diligence is an interesting word to study. It's a motivational word which means "get going!" Here is how the word diligence can be defined in modern terms:

"Get going,"

"Get on with it,"

"Waste no time,"

"Put feet on your dreams and run,"

"Activate your gifts,"

"Do something with your vision."

This word epitomizes high performance habits. Diligence is the opposite of procrastination; the reverse of laziness. It's a "do it now" kind of word. It's our first additive for high performance living.

Do you know what your mission in life is? Get on with it!

Have you identified your special gift from God? Do something NOW to fan the flame of it. Do something TODAY toward fulfilling the dream God has put in your heart. Diligence means to make an all out effort to add the things to your life that will make you a high performance believer.

As Dick pointed out in his word study, diligence combines two words: speed and skill. It means to act quickly, but skillfully. Some folks have speed with no skill. And others have skill but never seem to act quickly enough to get the benefit. Lightning, for example, has speed but no skill. It can wreak havoc and destruction everywhere it touches. There are believers like that. They move with a great deal of speed, but because of their lack of skill, they leave a messy trail wherever they go.

On the other hand, you see people with enormous skills who never act quickly enough to make a difference in their world. They're poky, like an old tugboat. They just chug-chug through life, hanging back, holding off, and refusing to launch out into the deep water. They move too slowly to get anywhere!

Diligence is additive number one. It means "GET ON WITH IT!"

Author Tom Peters did America a great service when he published his book *In Pursuit Of Excellence* in 1980. In the 1970's, our American industries had largely fallen into a "mediocrity mania," and the book seemed to jar the country back to a consciousness of the importance of quality and excellence in both workmanship and service. Peters elaborated on 43 of the country's best run companies. Unfortunately today, 14 of those 43 companies are in bad shape. They're struggling.

What happened? Well, according to Robert Tucker, author of *Managing the Future*, these companies either forgot, or ignored, the diligence additive. They moved too slowly to respond to the changing needs of the American people. The department stores, for example, once a mainstay of American culture, served the American housewife who had the leisure hours each week to browse and shop. But things changed. More and more women entered the work force and found less and less time for shopping. Specialty stores opened. Discount stores came on the scene. Appliance stores opened and took a whopping market share from the department stores. Convenience and speed became the keynote for the American shopper. Women no longer were willing to spend hours browsing for what they wanted to buy. They wanted to go in, find the merchandise, pay, and get out.

But many of the old department stores just continued on the way they had for years. Too slowly, they realized that the greatest part of their market share was gone. So they tried to play "catch up," and so far, have had little success in gaining back what they lost to the more convenient, quick service oriented stores. Gimbels has now vanished. Bloomingdales, Saks Fifth Avenue, Macy's, and other, once thriving department stores are all either bankrupt, up for sale, or struggling for their lives. They didn't move fast enough when America changed.

Think for a moment of the office supply stores that have been knocked out of the race by the new office products super stores. What about the neighborhood grocer who left the race when the mega-supermarkets opened. They had opportunities to meet the expanding and demanding needs of their customers, but they moved too slowly. Diligence — a "do it now" attitude — is a critical ingredient for high performance success. Diligence will provide for you an ability to make the best of any opportunity to grow, expand, develop, and prosper.

Let me illustrate what diligence can do for you and how it can work miracles. Years ago, I had a black walnut tree in my back yard. Have you ever tried to crack a black walnut shell? Well I have, and let me tell you, it's no easy task. I broke more than one nutcracker trying. In fact, one Christmas I bought my wife a beautiful nut basket with a built-in nutcracker. You guessed it. I broke that beautiful gift trying to crack open one of our walnuts. Finally, after trying everything I knew to get those nuts opened, I went down to the basement, set a nut on the floor, picked up a hammer, and smashed it to pieces. Little bits of shell embedded themselves in the meat of the nut making it impossible to eat.

Then, I planted one of those walnuts in the earth, and a miracle happened! That hard shelled nut sprouted and came up through the ground, eventually producing a little black walnut tree. I thought about that and realized that it had demonstrated the epitome of diligence. I had tried with brute force to crack the shell, with no success. Yet the nut, planted in the right conditions, softened in the sun-warmed earth. Then a tiny, flimsy sprout pushed through that tough shell, and there was no stopping it. What that little sprout did to the shell is what diligence can do for you. It can break the toughest situations of life. It can bring the miraculous into your life.

God has made some wonderful promises to people who cultivate the diligence habit. For example, in Exodus 15:26, He promised that those who diligently hearkened to His voice would be protected from the plagues suffered by the Egyptians. God has promised to preserve the diligent.

In Hebrews 6:11, He promised hope and vision for those who add diligence to their lives.

In Deuteronomy 11:14 and Hebrews 11:6, God offers special rewards for diligence.

In Proverbs 11:27, a special promise of favor is presented to the person of diligence.

Prosperity is also a promise for the person who has added diligence to his life as a habit pattern. Read Proverbs 10:4, 13:4, 12:24, and 22:29.

Chapter Eight

ENEMIES OF DILIGENCE

By Dave Williams

Just as there are hindrances to winning a race, like engine failure or a flat tire, there are enemies to the habit of diligence. Let's look at them.

■ **1. Lack of a sense of mission** — You are not placed on earth to merely check off days on the calendar. You are here on a mission from heaven. Wherever you go on this earth, you are on a mission. You can't escape it. You have an assignment from above. When you know your mission, you can focus your energies and move ahead. But how can you focus on something if you don't even know what that something is? You can't.

In marriage, each party has a mission in that relationship. My wife's mission is to fit in with my plans and take care of me as a helpmate. She's my partner. When she's fulfilling that mission, she's the happiest lady in town. When she's not, she's miserable. On the other hand, my mission in marriage is to cherish my wife and to lavish her with my love. When I'm not fulfilling my mission in marriage, I'm miserable (and she makes sure that I am).

My mission as a father is to train my children in the things of God and things that pertain to life. I am not to be a tormentor or frustrator to them, but a coach, a friend, and someone who can nourish them in spiritual things.

My staff has a mission. Their mission is to make my job easier. If they make it more difficult for me to pastor the church, they are miserable because they have failed their mission.

Jesus, Himself, had a mission. Do you know what Jesus' mission was? Well, I'm sure glad there weren't news commentators when Jesus walked the earth. Suppose there was a commentary that read, "Jesus had one purpose, and that purpose was to die." I've read that nonsense so many times. His mission was not merely to die. His mission was to destroy the works of the devil: sin, sickness, poverty, disease, and death. That was His mission. If His mission was "to die," He might as well have died when He was born, instead of suffering the pain of the cross.

"He that committeth sin is of the devil; for the devil sinneth from the beginning. For this purpose the Son

*of God was manifested, that He might
destroy the works of the devil."*

1 John 3:8

The cross was a step in the direction of fulfilling His mission, but it was not the mission. Do you see why it is so important to know what our mission is? We get confused between means and ends, and the whats and the hows. The mission is the "what." The Father said, "Jesus, go to earth. Become one of them. Live a sinless life, and destroy the works of the devil." The cross was the means of accomplishing that goal — the destruction of Satan's malignant works. But that's not the end of the story.

The third day He rose from the dead and later ascended into heaven and said, "I'm coming back to get you." By the signs all around us, He may be coming back real soon. But His mission was to destroy the works of the devil. "Tell the bound that they don't have to be bound any more; tell the sick they don't have to be sick any more; tell the poor they don't have to be poor; tell the lost they don't have to be lost," was Jesus' message to us. He knew His mission.

Why not invest some time finding your special mission in life? It will help prevent you from expending valuable energy on diffused activities. Pray. Ask the Lord about your life's mission. Find your special ministry and gifts, then use them to fulfill your mission.

■ **2. Lack of organization** — The mission is the "what." Organization of it is the "how." It takes diligence to organize a mission. I know what my mission is. My challenge is how to achieve it. So, I sit down and prayerfully organize by planning, scheduling, and preparing.

■ **3. Indecision** — Does this sound like you in the morning? "Oh, what will I wear today? I'll try this on. This is a little tight. I don't think I'll wear this today." Or, how about at the restaurant? "Let's see, I don't know if I want the fish, or the hamburger, or the patty melt. Oh, the chicken looks good. 'Could you give me a few more minutes, I'm still deciding. Well, maybe the steak. Chocolate cake or peach pie? Do you use real or powdered potatoes?'" Do you see what I mean? Indecision wastes time and is a symptom of unfocused thinking. Learn to make up your mind.

■ **4. Lack of concentration** — This is one of the most important principles of time management: focusing on one thing at a time. We have a saying around my office, "Winners focus: losers spray."

■ **5. Procrastination** — Procrastination is the reverse of diligence. It has its root in laziness.

There you have it — two kinds of believers and two kinds of entrances into heaven. There are two kinds of habit patterns that reveal what kind of believer we're going to be and what kind of entrance we'll have into heaven. Now, let me share with you a poem. To my mind, it neatly illustrates the difference between a champion and one who "also ran."

> *"The average runner sprints*
> *until the breath in him is gone.*
> *But the champion has a diligent will*
> *that makes him carry on.*
> *For rest the average runner begs*
> *when limp his muscles grow.*
> *But the champion runs on leadened legs,*
> *his diligence makes them go.*
> *The average man's complacent*
> *when he's done his best to score.*
> *But the champion does his best*
> *and then he does a little more."*
> *— Author unknown*

Don't let reward and honor escape you in this life or the next. Add diligence to your life today. Think of one thing that needs action now...and do it!

Chapter Nine
ADDITIVE #2: FAITH — PISTIS
"SET IN MOTION" WORD
By Dick Mills

In the Bible, faith is a very illustrious and distinctive word. "Faith" is the New Testament word for the Old Testament word "trust." Faith has so many rich possibilities; it is not easy to define. Yet it is the foundation word that sets in motion all other Christian activity.

"Faith" in the Greek is the word PISTIS. The word is very similar in pronunciation to pistol and piston. Looking in Strong's, #4102, you will notice three other similar words: "Pisteuo"— to believe or put your trust in a person or a thing; "Pistos"— faithful or trustworthy; and "Pistoo"— to assure/reassure or cause someone to trust.

Universally, faith (PISTIS) is the religious belief of Christians. When it relates to the Heavenly Father, faith becomes a conviction that God exists and is the Creator and Ruler of all things. Faith acknowledges that God the Father provided for us and bestowed upon us eternal salvation through His son, Jesus Christ (Thayer).

In reference to Christ, faith (PISTIS) produces a strong and welcome conviction that Jesus is the Messiah, through whom we obtain eternal salvation in the Kingdom of God (Thayer).

Some Bible scholars liken faith to a soil that all other Christian virtues and graces can thrive and grow in. Biggs, in the ICC calls faith "the heavenly germ which is fostered by obedience and issues in love." A.T. Robertson calls PISTIS "the root of the Christian life." He states that "faith is the foundation that goes through various steps up to love."

William Barclay links faith to the promises of God. He defines PISTIS as "Unquestioning certainty that the way to happiness, peace, and strength on earth and in heaven is to accept God at His word."

Faith is recognized by the action it produces. Faith is a word that is both passive and active. Souter defines faith (PISTIS) as "The leaning of the entire human personality upon God or the Messiah in absolute trust and confidence in His power, wisdom, and goodness." We are told in 1 John 5:4 that, "This is the victory that overcomes the world, even our faith." Can faith be reduced to percentages? Can we have half faith, partial faith, ten percent, or ninety percent faith? I hardly think so. However, we do find these words in scripture, "Great faith, little faith, and no faith."

It is interesting that faith is the only word used in all three clusters: the Fruit of the Spirit, the Giftings of the Spirit, and the additives of the Spirit life. It is the one ingredient Jesus will be especially looking for in all of us at His second coming according to Luke 18:8.

"FAITH"

TRANSLATIONS

Of all the translations consulted, only one did not use the word "*faith.*" A. Cressman substituted the word "*believe*" instead.

"Faith is the living, divinely implanted acquired and created principle of inward and whole hearted confidence, assurance, trust and reliance in God and all that He says."

—Finis Dake

Chapter Ten
FAITH: THE MAIN INGREDIENT
By Dave Williams

My mother used to make the best cookies in town. They were at least seven inches in diameter — as I remember them — and were made from my favorite ingredients. Oatmeal, raisins, walnuts, and chocolate chips had to go in, with powdered sugar sprinkled over the top. Everybody in the neighborhood raved over them, and in my mind, they will always be the best cookies ever made.

I loved those cookies. Every ingredient was essential to making a successful batch. One time she forgot the salt, just a small component, but the cookies just weren't the same. They tasted flat. Blah! We ended up feeding them to the neighborhood dogs.

Yes, all the ingredients in a recipe are essential, but every recipe has a starting point, that main ingredient that is first into the bowl, and to which all of the other ingredients are added. In my mother's cookies, the main ingredient was flour. In the life of a Christian, the main ingredient is faith. In 2 Peter 1:5, we are told, "...giving all diligence, add to your faith..." all the rest of the spiritual additives that turn a lackluster spiritual life into a life filled with miracles and victory, rich with the fulfillment of God's promises!

Before we delve too deeply into the subject of personal faith and the miracles that will be released once we exercise personal faith in our lives, we must first discuss the most essential faith that every person must have. Salvation faith is the flour, the main ingredient, in the successful Christian recipe.

Until a person comes to Christ, he remains lost. He is not in "the faith." No matter how moral or good he may try to be, inevitably he will be corrupted. Sooner or later it always happens. He may try to turn over a new leaf. He may practice the highest levels of self-discipline and self-control; but regardless of how high a pinnacle of morality or "religion" he reaches, if he is separated from the cross of Christ, and the One who died on that cross, he is still in a state of sin.

R.A. Torrey was talking with a doctor one day. This man was a moral, decent person — a "good" man. Torrey asked him, "Doctor, are you born again?" "No, I do not describe myself as being born again. However, I am a decent human being; I try to do my best. I feel that is enough," he responded.

Torrey then drew a square on a piece of paper and said, "Doctor, this square represents the state of Colorado. The highest mountain, Pike's Peak, is 14,200 feet above sea level. The ground level in Colorado is 2,000 feet above sea level, and then there are the deep mines. There are men working down in those mines as deep as 3,000 feet below sea level! Let me ask you, what state are all of them in?"

"The state of Colorado," answered the doctor.

"You're exactly right," Torrey responded. "And no matter how deep into the mines and caverns of wickedness, perversion, and flagrant transgression someone goes; and no matter how high someone climbs the 'Mount of Morality' or the 'Ridge of Religion,' he is in the same state until he changes states. There is only one way to change states. That is to throw yourself at the foot of the cross and say, 'Jesus, I can't make it by myself. I need a Savior.'"

That is why it's so important to bring our loved ones and friends into salvation faith. They may be good people. They may be trying their best. We may think, "How can God send such a good person to hell when they die?" The answer is simple. God doesn't send good people to hell. They choose to go because they never had faith in the biggest promise God ever made to humanity — the promise of salvation through the blood of Jesus Christ. God offers this simple provision of salvation and eternal life to everyone — good and bad.

Today we see a phenomenon I call "designer religion." This is a smorgasbord approach to religion. It is seen frequently among "Baby Busters." These are people born between 1964 and 1984. They are the children of the "Baby Boomers" and are the first generation raised primarily by the television. They have parents, but their values, education, and moral training come mainly from TV, the electronic babysitter for their busy parents. These are the children that have grown up with music videos and horror movies. They received no real moral training in public schools, and mom and dad usually found little time for church or Sunday school. Forty percent grew up with only one parent. Many struggled with stepparents and stepbrothers or stepsisters.

"Baby Busters," in general, believe that everything is broken. They are a generation of the hopeless. The future is bleak to them. They search for meaning in their lives, but without direction, they end up developing their own philosophies. "Baby Busters" will visit a church and say, "Yeah, Jesus is cool." So they add a little Jesus into the mix. Then they visit a New Age occult meeting and glean a few ideas from there. "Let's add a little transcendental meditation and a dab of Eastern mysticism." Soon they've cooked up their own philosophy. It seems good to them. But they are deluded.

It's like a free for all, everyone doing their own thing. But they never come into real salvation by faith in Jesus Christ. Until they accept Jesus as their Savior, and the full body of God's truth as found in His Word, the Bible; they only have a form of "religion." The question isn't whether they have religion. The question is, "Do they have Jesus?"

Once we have salvation through faith in Jesus, the whole spectrum of God's promises are open to us. Every day we face struggles and problems. And for every struggle and every problem we encounter, there is a promise and a solution in God's Word. Armed with our faith and diligently seeking to exercise and grow in our personal faith, we can search the Word for His promises. Now let us learn of the wonders of personal faith; let's see what it can do for us.

Chapter Eleven
PERSONAL FAITH
By Dave Williams

Now that we know what it means to be in "the faith," through belief in Christ's completed work on the cross, let's go on to discover the amazing riches of personal faith. Some do not like the term "personal faith." They declare that all faith is from God; therefore, there is no such thing as personal faith. But when Jesus spoke to people who had received miracles, He often said, "Your faith has made you whole." What is "your faith?" It's personal faith. In this chapter, we'll begin looking at the miracle substance of personal faith.

Every day we face struggles. Perhaps you're struggling today with a sickness. Or maybe you're struggling to pay your bills. Maybe you have trouble in your relationships and are looking for answers. It's a fact of life; we all face problems and challenges every day. But God has a precious promise for every struggle we are facing today or will ever face in the future. He has the solution and has promised to meet our needs and desires.

"But my God shall supply all your need according to His riches in glory by Christ Jesus."

Philippians 4:19

"The fear of the wicked, it shall come upon him: but the desire of the righteous shall be granted."

Proverbs 10:24

"Therefore I say unto you, What things soever ye desire, when ye pray, believe that ye receive them, and ye shall have them."

Mark 11:24

But how do we get those wonderful promises off the pages of God's Word and into our lives where we need them? The answer is faith. Faith is the main substance of the Christian life which activates all the promises of God.

Think about this. A promise will never become a reality until it is appropriated by faith. Suppose I promised my wife a new coat and told her that it was at the store waiting for her to go and pick up. If she had no faith in me, no belief that what I told her was true, she would not go and pick up the coat. So even though the coat was there, waiting for her to enjoy, it would do her no good. But my wife believes in me; she knows I don't lie. She would immediately go to the store and claim her coat. That is faith in action. Faith hears a promise, believes the promise, and acts upon the promise to claim it for its own.

People take different approaches to God for getting their needs met. One may try pleading with God, whining and crying hot tears. Another may beg abjectly. Someone else may seek to convince God of their worthiness to receive by recounting all their good deeds. Still another may search for methods of manipulating God to meet their needs.

I heard about a young boy who wanted a new bicycle, so he set out to convince God to give him one. He started a letter to God, "Dear God, I've been a good boy all my life...." Suddenly he remembered, God knows everything. So he wadded up the note and threw it away. He tried again, "Dear God, I've been a good boy most of my life." He realized even that statement missed the mark of truthfulness, so he gave up on the letter writing idea.

One day, while he was out playing with his little Catholic friend, they passed by the Catholic church where there stood a statue of Mary. "Who's that," he inquired of his friend.

"Oh, she's the mother of God," responded the Catholic boy.

Late that night while everyone else was sleeping, the little fellow crawled out of bed, went to the window of his bedroom with a blanket, and climbed out quietly. He went to the garage and got his wagon, placed the blanket in it and headed for the Catholic church. When he arrived, he carefully wrapped the statue of Mary in his blanket, tipped her into the wagon, and took her home. After hoisting the statue into his bedroom, he began another letter to God.

"Dear God, if you ever wanna see your mother again, You better get me that new bike!" I don't need to tell you that this is not the way to receive from God.

What moves the hand of God on our behalf? Low performance believers use the unfruitful methods of pleading, begging, crying, manipulating, pouting, threatening, and trying to convince God. High performance believers have discovered the truth. They have learned that there is only one thing that moves the hand of God on their behalf: Faith!

Chapter Twelve

WHAT IS FAITH? WHO HAS IT?

By Dave Williams

Faith is the substance — the essential ingredient — for receiving anything from God.

Faith is the evidence that the promise is on the way, even though unseen by human eye and unheard by human ear.

> *"Now faith is the substance of things hoped for, the evidence of things not seen...But without faith it is impossible to please Him: for he that cometh to God must believe that He is, and that He is a rewarder of them that diligently seek Him."*
>
> *Hebrews 11:1,6*

Let me ask you a question. If God gave you the choice between $5 million in cash or unlimited opportunities to develop strong faith, which would you choose? The children of Israel faced similar choices in their journeys. They got what they asked for, but leanness came to their souls (Psalm 106:15). Because they desired material blessings over the life of faith, they lost wars, their sick died, confusion and chaos came to their lives.

Faith can bring money, but money can't bring faith. Through faith we can reach into the unseen world and pull whatever it is we need into the natural, visible world. Faith gives us access to the supply house of heaven. Banks may collapse on earth, but our treasuries in heaven shall never have a shortage. The bank of heaven is always solvent and has more than enough!

WHO HAS FAITH?

The Bible gives us many examples of the infinite possibilities of faith. In fact, everything that was promised to Abraham also belongs to everyone who has faith in Jesus Christ. Every blessing Abraham enjoyed, we too can enjoy. Faith gives substance to invisible hopes. But where do we get this miracle working substance called faith?

First, everyone is born with some measure of natural faith. Children, for example, believe they can do almost anything.

When I was three years old, I believed I could fly. After all, if Peter Pan could fly, so could I. So, without my mother's knowledge, I climbed onto the garage roof. My horrified mother glanced out the back window just in time to see me jump and smash to the ground. My childlike faith had misled me, but by God's grace I only had the wind knocked out of me. I could have been killed! Children have a natural capacity for believing things — sometimes the wrong things.

That is why Paul told believers to quit acting like children, tossed to and fro with every new wind of doctrine. In other words, be mature and believe the right things. My point is, all of us are born with some capacity for faith. Natural faith may get you into the boat, but it can never cause you to walk on water. Only supernatural faith can do that.

To the born again believer, one who is in "the faith," God has already imparted an adequate measure of faith — supernatural faith — to start with.

> *"For I say, through the grace given unto me, to every man that is among you, not to think of himself more highly than he ought to think; but to think soberly, according as God hath dealt to every man the measure of faith."*
>
> *Romans 12:3*

Once we have faith imparted to us, we can develop it. We know this is true because the Bible talks about dead faith, weak faith, and strong faith. From this we know there are different measures of faith. Faith is dead when the possessor of it never acts upon it. Weak faith believes God but is more apt to pray and cry about a problem than to take God at His Word and act on God's promises. For example, when the storm struck the disciples' boat and the waves roared and the wind howled, they all cried out in fear. But Jesus got up confidently and rebuked the winds. He then turned to the disciples and remarked, "Oh, ye of little faith." They could have just as easily spoken to the storm and halted it as Jesus had.

Faith must be developed. Romans 10:17 tells us that faith cometh. That means it appears and is developed by hearing the Word. You can't pray for faith. You can't even say you don't have enough faith. You have all the faith you need. It just may require some developing.

If a person owned 1000 acres of land but there was no place to build a ranch, he could say, "I need more property." But in reality, more property is not what he really needs. He just needs to develop the property he already has. The same is true with faith. We have all the faith we need for anything we need to accomplish, but we may need to develop what we have. Nobody has a faith problem; some just have a development problem. The way to develop faith is to increase our intake of God's Word. Faith is developed by hearing God's Word, hiding it in our hearts, and verbally articulating the precious promises as our personal own.

Another important truth to understand in cultivating faith is the fact that Jesus Christ is the agent of faith's development.

> *"Looking unto Jesus the author*
> *and finisher of our faith; who for the*
> *joy that was set before Him endured*
> *the cross, despising the shame, and*
> *is set down at the right hand of the*
> *throne of God."*
>
> *Hebrews 12:2*

Faith can be developed, refined, and honed to a razor's edge. Jesus takes the Word we put into us and uses it to develop our faith.

Does it all sound like sheer fantasy? Is faith really the answer for receiving anything we need from God? Does faith really bring us unlimited possibilities? Stop and think for a moment. What do you need today? What do you want today? Do you have a deep desire to be a high performance believer? Faith is the main ingredient. Now, let's look at some of God's promises and what faith can do.

Chapter Thirteen

WHAT FAITH CAN DO

By Dave Williams

Faith is the master key to heaven's treasuries. It unlocks, releases, and activates all the promises of God. Without faith, we'd never see heaven. Without faith, we'd never experience miracles. Without faith, our lives would go unprotected. Peter reminds us that God has given exceedingly great and precious promises. And these promises are just waiting for the person of faith to grab hold of them.

Let's look at one chapter of the Bible. It's often called the "faith chapter," Hebrews, Chapter eleven. In this chapter we are shown the manifold spiritual blessings derived from faith.

■ 1. It can bring us righteousness (verse 4).

■ 2. It caused Enoch to be supernaturally transported (verse 5).

■ 3. Faith pleases God (verse 6).

■ 4. It brought blessings to Jacob's children (verse 21).

■ 5. It caused Rahab, a harlot, to be saved (verse 31).

■ 6. Faith is the ingredient that obtains promises (verse 33).

Hebrews Chapter eleven also describes how faith brings miracles.

■ 1. Faith made Abraham and Sarah parents when they were too old to have children (verse 11).

■ 2. Faith caused the dead to be raised to life (verse 35).

■ 3. Faith brought freedom to God's people in Egypt through the fantastic miracles wrought by Moses (verse 29).

Faith can also bring victories even when defeat looks inevitable.

■ 1. Faith saved Noah and his family from the flood (verse 7).

■ 2. Faith caused the defeat of enemies (verse 30).

■ 3. Faith subdued kingdoms (verse 33).

■ 4. Faith quenched violence (verse 34).

■ 5. Faith brought a great escape from trouble (verse 34).

■ 6. Faith turned weakness into strength (verse 34).

■ 7. Faith caused armies to have mighty courage (verse 34).

These are just a few of the benefits of faith. With faith, no problem is insurmountable, no trial too difficult, no dream impossible. Faith will provide you with more stamina, more resiliency, and more radiance. Faith makes all your problems exciting opportunities to see God working His miracles in your life.

FAITH BRINGS PROTECTION

God has promised to protect us. But remember, promises must be acted upon in faith if we want to see the benefits of them.

Some time ago, a judge's office was bombed. He was killed instantly. A few weeks later, the office of a political action group was bombed. The leader was killed. Then not long after that, the daughter of a well-known pastor opened a package sent to the ministry, and it exploded. The entire office was in ruins. The back of the chair in which she was sitting was blown completely out. But she lived. In fact, she had only a few minor burns! The bomb experts said, "It's a miracle." Yes, it was a miracle of God's protection.

FAITH BRINGS HEALING

Faith brings healing. Read the amazing healings that took place in the Bible. Do you think those healing blessings were just for people in the Bible? Wrong! Jesus Christ is the same yesterday, today, and forever. He still heals today. But to receive healing, faith must be released against the sickness.

One morning I was so sick, I could barely stay awake as my wife and I prayed. It was Sunday, and I was expected to preach three times that day. I have never missed a time in the pulpit due to illness, but I wondered if this might be the first. I felt terrible. My throat was so sore; I could barely talk. I was committed to preach though, so my wife and I stood on God's healing promises, and we agreed in prayer on Matthew 18:19. I didn't feel like going to church to preach. I felt like crawling into a hole somewhere and croaking. But I possessed the promise, spoke the Word, and acted upon it by confessing the promise and not the problem.

So, I shivered through my shower, dragged on my clothes, and drove to church. All the time I wondered if I would have to pull over to the side of the road — my head throbbed, my throat burned, and my stomach rolled like a boat on high seas. But I clung to my faith and continued to confess God's healing in this situation.

Then a miracle occurred. When I arrived at the church, pulled into my parking spot, and walked through the doors, I noticed that, suddenly, I felt great! The headache was gone, my throat felt fine, and my stomach was calm again. I was able to preach a powerful message that day, thanks to God, and over forty people accepted Jesus Christ that morning. What if I had caved into the "reality" of my senses and stayed home? Suppose I had just prayed when I was sick and said, "If it's Your will to heal me, just come down with Your healing gun and shoot me with a dose." That is not putting faith into action; that is just empty talk. Faith has to be acted upon for us to receive the benefit or the blessing.

Praise God, faith can bring healing to a sick body. The devil is a terrorist. He will try to terrorize you with violence, sickness, disease, sin, guilt, discouragement, depression, and lies. And this is just a partial list of his tricks! But the tool that will protect us against all his nefarious attempts to snare us is faith. Faith will stop the devil in his tracks.

One evening I wanted to teach my children a lesson in grace. I took $10 and held it up to my daughter and said, "Honey, I know you did something you shouldn't have this week, but here's $10 I'd like to give you anyway." She responded, "Oh dad, I can't take that."

So I held it up to my son and said, "David, I don't know if you've done anything bad this week or not, but I want you to have this $10." He grabbed it out of my hand so fast, I hadn't even finished my sentence. That was faith. Taking action to grab something I had offered. When my daughter saw her brother's faith, it inspired her to take $10 from me too. Out of my love for them, I wanted to give my children something for no reason other than to bless them. I offered it to them, but they had to take it.

God's blessings are like that too. When He hands us a promise, we must reach out with faith action and take it. What do you need today? A miracle? Deliverance? An idea? What is it? Find the promise in God's Word and take it by faith. You will find that you will move from victory to victory in your quest to become a high performance believer.

Chapter Fourteen
ENEMIES OF YOUR FAITH - 1
By Dave Williams

Paul instructed young Timothy to "fight the good fight of faith." If there is a fight to be fought, it is because there are enemies of faith. These enemies come in disguise and stand ready to thwart your success. Now let's look at eight big enemies of faith. First, read the faith account of Abraham.

> *"And the father of circumcision to them who are not of the circumcision only, but who also walk in the steps of that faith of our father Abraham, which he had being yet uncircumcised. For the promise, that he should be the heir of the world, was not to Abraham, or to his seed, through the law, but through the righteousness of faith. For if they which are of the law be heirs, faith is*

made void, and the promise made of none effect: Because the law worketh wrath: for where no law is, there is no transgression. Therefore it is of faith, that it might be by grace; to the end the promise might be sure to all the seed; not to that only which is of the law, but to that also which is of the faith of Abraham; who is the father of us all, (As it is written, I have made thee a father of many nations,) before him whom he believed, even God, who quickeneth the dead, and calleth those things which be not as though they were. Who against hope believed in hope, that he might become the father of many nations, according to that which was spoken, So shall thy seed be. And being not weak in faith, he considered not his own body now dead, when he was about an hundred years old, neither yet the deadness of Sarah's womb: He staggered not at the promise of God through unbelief; but was strong in faith, giving glory to God; And being fully persuaded that, what he had promised, he was able also to perform. And therefore it was imputed to him for righteousness. Now it was not written for his sake alone, that it was imputed to him;

But for us also, to whom it shall be imputed, if we believe on him that raised up Jesus our Lord from the dead; Who was delivered for our offences, and was raised again for our justification."

Romans 4:12-25

■ **Enemy No. 1 — Not understanding that faith is a process.** In other words, there are definite steps to releasing your faith. For example, how do you get from the first floor to the second floor? Do you jump up in one giant leap? No. You will never make it, and more likely you'll probably fall. Does that mean that you can never get from the first floor to the second floor because you can't jump there? Of course not. You simply need to use the steps which are always provided. Take one step at a time. Read Romans 4:12-25. It talks about steps of faith. Let's look at those steps.

Step One — Get God's Word on the matter first. Find a promise that covers your need. Don't be swayed by the voice of man. Remember it was man who said, "The Titanic is unsinkable." But it sunk. Do you need help with your finances? Get God's Word on the matter. Don't waste time and money going to a financial seminar. See what God says about money and your finances first. Do you need a healing for your body? Find God's Word on the matter. Do you need a miracle? What is it that you need from God? Get His Word — His promise — first.

Step Two — Speak faith words according to God's Word. Speak the promise, not the problem. Faith words seem to activate creative forces that go to work on your behalf. Jonathan and his aide conquered an entire company of Philistine soldiers by using faith words, words in harmony with God's will. Once you have God's Word on a matter, speak it. Never allow your senses or your situation to dictate what the words of your mouth will be.

Step Three — Make a faith movie. This is what I call "hope." Faith is the substance of things you hope for. Hope is a picture of the end result of receiving a promise of God. If you have found a promise of healing for your body, and you have boldly spoken what God's promise says concerning your healing, then get hope working for you by "seeing" that promise come true with your eye of faith. Produce an internal movie starring you after the promise is realized. See yourself as if the Word of God has already been fulfilled in your life. I call this a "faith movie."

Step Four — Exercise your praise muscles. Praise God in advance for what He is doing, according to His Word, in your life. Praise Him for the answer to your problem. You have His Word; you are speaking it daily and seeing yourself as the recipient of God's promise. So thank and praise God ahead of time. Do it now.

Step Five — Take action! When Peter told the crippled man at the Gate Beautiful to rise up and walk, the man had to do something. He had to take action to receive his miracle. When Jesus told a blind man to go wash in the pool of Siloam, the man had to take action. You'll see the same principle in every Bible incident where faith brought a great victory. Some people say, "I'm living by faith." They may be professing the Word of God and seeing themselves in light of the promises of God, but they're not taking action. Laziness will never get you anything from God. Faith + Action = Results.

Step Six — Patience. Patient endurance is the bridge between believing a promise from God and receiving the promise from God. Tenacity. Hanging-in-there power. Look at the life of David. In his faith ventures, he used all six steps. For instance, when the Philistine giant was taunting and threatening the people of Israel, David found God's promise, spoke it boldly, saw himself slicing off the head of that giant, praised God, took action, and didn't give up until the giant's body lay lifeless on the ground. Faith has steps.

■ **Enemy No. 2 — Not having a specific promise from God.** (Read verses 16 and 17 of Romans Chapter four). Too many times I've heard somebody say, "I'm standing on the Word." I've started asking people, "What Word?" Usually they'll start mumbling and jumbling to find an answer. They respond by saying, "Oh, uh, God's Word. That's what I'm standing on." Well, that's so ambiguous, they might as well pull out their King James Version, put it on the floor, and literally stand on it. It will do just about as much good as just saying, "I'm standing on the Word."

For faith to function, it must have a specific word, a concrete promise from the Bible. The specific promise then becomes a target for faith. Jesus said, "You do err not knowing the Scriptures or the power of God." A great error among many believers is to stand upon the general Word of God rather than a specific promise when trying to exercise faith. Remember, your goal is to be a high performance believer, and high performance believers have learned to focus their faith for miracle results. Focus begins with a firm promise from God.

One day I was attacked by the spirit of fear. It started out as a simple little worry. Rather than resisting it, I allowed it to persist. Soon my mind was paralyzed with fear. I literally couldn't think. My faith was neutralized — short-circuited. I prayed but it didn't help. I tried praising God, but that didn't help either. Then I got out my Bible and found some promises and began to write them out on a piece of paper. As I focused on those promises, faith welled up in me; and as it did, fear was driven out!

When Jesus faced the devil in the wilderness, He drove him out with simple, specific words from the Father. You can do the same. Always obtain an unconditional promise from God's Word before trying to muster up enough faith for miracle results.

■ **Enemy No. 3 — Not understanding the power of God** (see verse 17). With God, nothing is impossible! The power of God did not die out with the last apostle. One of God's biggest complaints against His people was, "They limited the Holy One of Israel." How did God's people limit Him? By their unbelief in His power. God went on to say, that had they understood His power and willingness to do "impossible things" on their behalf, they would have been able to ask for anything, and the request would have been fulfilled.

We often confine or restrict God to our puny abilities. We limit Him to our own bank accounts. We can make our plans one of two ways. One, we can check our own resources, find out what we can do, and plan accordingly. Or two, we can step up to a new dimension of high performance living and make our plans based upon what God said He will do for us and through us. God used birds to feed one of his prophets. Imagine, birds delivering pizza. Sounds funny doesn't it? I know of a missionary who had been craving some American ice cream. It had been so long since he and his family had tasted the treat they loved back home. One night, he opened the door of his home in Africa and found on the stoop a gallon container of his favorite brand of chocolate ice cream. They were stunned but greatly blessed and enjoyed the treat thoroughly.

At the same time, something strange was happening back in the United States. Some dear friends of the African missionary were on a diet and were craving something sweet. They remembered how much their friends loved ice cream, so they convinced themselves to buy some chocolate ice cream and eat it in their honor — a tricky way to cheat on a diet! So they went to the store and then headed home with the taboo treat. But when they arrived home and opened their trunk, the gallon of chocolate ice cream was gone. It had disappeared! Did God, knowing the couple was about to break their diet, send an angel to take it and deliver it to the African missionaries who were longing for a taste of home?

The American couple and the missionary family shared this strange tale when next they met and discovered that the day the ice cream was missing from the trunk in America was the same day it showed up on the front step in Africa. Did God do one couple a favor by saving them the fat grams, and at the same time, reward the other family in His service?

Can this story be true? Can God supernaturally transport ice cream? Our disbelief is a measure of our willingness to limit the power of God. When you read the story, — which is true — did your belief mechanism say, "No way?" Or did you sense something leap in you, saying, "Praise God, He is bigger and more powerful than my mind can conceive!" Your response shows how much you understand and believe in the power of God.

Chapter Fifteen

ENEMIES OF YOUR FAITH - 2

By Dave Williams

Let's examine the life of Abraham more closely now. We're spending more time on the subject of faith because it's the main ingredient of the high performance additives.

"(As it is written, I have made thee a father of many nations,) before him whom he believed, even God, who quickeneth the dead, and calleth those things which be not as though they were. Who against hope believed in hope, that he might become the father of many nations, according to that which was spoken, So shall thy seed be. And being not weak in faith, he considered not his own body now dead, when he was about an hundred years old, neither

> *yet the deadness of Sarah's womb:*
> *He staggered not at the promise of*
> *God through unbelief; but was*
> *strong in faith, giving glory to God;*
> *And being fully persuaded that,*
> *what He had promised, He was able*
> *also to perform."*
>
> *Romans 4:17-21*

What does it say about faith in these verses?

■ 1. Abraham received a promise from God.

■ 2. God can bring even the dead to life. If you need a miracle like resurrection (or something less miraculous), God can do it without any effort at all.

■ 3. Faith calls things that are not yet as though they already are.

■ 4. Abraham hoped when there was no obvious reason to hope.

■ 5. Abraham was not weak in faith.

■ 6. He did not consider the situation, only the promise.

■ 7. He did not stagger at God's promise through unbelief.

■ 8. He gave glory to God before the answer came.

■ 9. He was fully persuaded that what God had promised, He could, and would, perform.

In the previous chapter, we looked at three enemies of faith:

■ 1. Not understanding that faith is a process.

■ 2. Not having a specific promise from God for your situation.

■ 3. Not understanding the power of God.

Now let's discuss more enemies of your faith.

> *"Let us therefore fear, lest, a promise being left us of entering into His rest, any of you should seem to come short of it. For unto us was the gospel preached, as well as unto them: but the word preached did not profit them, not being mixed with faith in them that heard it. For we which have believed do enter into rest, as He said, As I have sworn in My wrath, if they shall enter into my rest: although the works were finished from the foundation of the world."*
>
> *Hebrews 4:1-3*

> *"Seeing therefore it remaineth that some must enter therein, and they to whom it was first preached entered not in because of unbelief."*
>
> *Hebrews 4:6*

> *"Let us labour therefore to en-*
> *ter into that rest, lest any man fall*
> *after the same example of unbelief."*
>
> Hebrews 4:11

■ **Enemy No. 4 — Unbelief or disbelief.** There are actually two Greek words which are translated "unbelief" in the King James Version. One word is UN-belief. The other is DIS-belief. They have different meanings.

Let's look at the difference. Unbelief is the absence of faith but doesn't necessarily deny the truth. Disbelief denies the truth blatantly. For example, if I said, "You must be born again to see the kingdom of heaven," and you responded by saying, "I don't believe that one bit." That's disbelief. Now unbelief says, "I believe that's true," but then never commits to Jesus. Disbelief expresses itself in disobedience; whereas unbelief expresses itself in lack of obedient action. Unbelief may understand a promise but will do nothing about it.

Disbelief denies the truth, and the effect is disobedience. Unbelief acknowledges the truth but doesn't act like the truth is relevant; therefore, it forfeits the promise of God. Both disbelief and unbelief result in the same thing: God is dishonored, and the promise is forfeited.

Let's look at another example. In 2 Corinthians 5:17, the Bible tells us, "...If any man be in Christ, he is a new creature: old things are passed away; behold, all things are become new." Whenever we say, "I believe that," but continue to act according to the old life, we are in unbelief. In 1 Peter 2:24, it says that by Christ's stripes (bruises) we were healed. Disbelief says, "I don't believe that." Unbelief is more dangerous because it says, "I believe that," but continues acting like it feels rather than by what God's Word says. Again, the promise is forfeited.

Whenever I quote 3 John 2, "Beloved, I wish above all things that thou mayest prosper and be in health, even as thy soul prospereth," invariably someone will say to me, "Brother Dave, I don't believe in that 'health and wealth' stuff." Disbelief doesn't see the promise. Unbelief turns its back on the promise.

Three things occur when unbelief is present. First, our ability to receive from God is limited.

> *"And He could there do no mighty work, save that He laid his hands upon a few sick folk, and healed them. And He marvelled because of their unbelief. And He went round about the villages, teaching."*
>
> *Mark 6:5-6*

> *"And He did not many mighty works there because of their unbelief."*
>
> *Matthew 13:58*

Can you imagine that? Incarnate Deity could not do any mighty miracles because of unbelief among the people. John Wesley stated, "God does nothing except in answer to believing prayer." Unbelief blocks the sole channel through which God's power can flow. Look at this:

> *"Yea, they turned back and tempted God, and limited the Holy One of Israel."*
>
> *Psalm 78:41*

It is possible to limit God. Unbelief is responsible for the seeming inactivity of God.

Second, where there is unbelief, there also is fear. Mark 4:40 connects fear with unbelief.

> *"And He said unto them, Why are ye so fearful? How is it that ye have no faith?"*
>
> *Mark 4:40*

Fear cannot be expelled by an act of will. It can be removed only by unwavering confidence in the love and power of God.

Third, when unbelief is working, all spiritual power is paralyzed.

> *"Then came the disciples to Jesus apart, and said, Why could not we cast him out? And Jesus said unto them, Because of your unbelief: for verily I say unto you, If ye*

*have faith as a grain of mustard
seed, ye shall say unto this mountain, Remove hence to yonder place;
and it shall remove; and nothing
shall be impossible unto you."*

Matthew 17:19-20

Jesus had given them all authority, but now in the presence of satanic forces, they were impotent. Why? They had
turned from faith in God's promise to faith in self. In essence, unbelief.

Unbelief blocks the only channel through which God
works in human lives. That channel is faith. Picture faith as
a television channel. That's something we can all understand. You receive the signal for channel six on channel six.
You do not receive the channel six signal on channel twelve.
The same way, God transmits answers to prayer on His faith
channel. If you are tuned in to the unbelief channel or the
disbelief channel, you never receive the miracles you need.
They are transmitted only on the faith channel.

It amazes me that our omnipotent God can be limited
by our unbelief and disbelief.

Don't let unbelief or disbelief rob you of God's best
for your life. Think of all the possibilities of faith. Faith is
that substance which enables us to get hold of the invisible realm. It enables us to treat the future as the present,
the unseen as seen. Faith is just as much at home in the
realm of the impossible as it is in the realm of the possible.

Faith relies on a God who knows no limitations, except those imposed by unbelief or disbelief. Faith grows through exercise, but atrophies through neglect. Faith is the power which turns promises into realities.

In the next chapter, we will look at more enemies of your faith.

Chapter Sixteen
ENEMIES OF YOUR FAITH - 3
By Dave Williams

Have you ever thought much about hope? You hear people say, "I hope things turn out all right," or "I hope I can make it." The truth is, most people, even Christians, do not have an adequate understanding of what Bible hope really is. That brings us to the next enemy of faith.

■ **Enemy No. 5 — Not understanding the role of hope.** Faith cannot function without hope.

> *"Now faith is the substance of things hoped for, the evidence of things not seen."*
>
> Hebrews 11:1

Hope is the image which faith sets out to achieve. It is like a blueprint. I like to call hope "the faith forecast." It is the future, seen by faith in the present. Bible hope is like a "faith movie" that you produce inside yourself. You base the script on God's Word, the Bible, and your God-given dreams. Then you "see" yourself succeeding.

Many fail because they "see" themselves as failing. Many struggle because they "see" themselves as struggling. They are victims of negative hope.

Jesus instructed His disciples in Bible hope when He said to them,

> *"Lift up your EYES; and LOOK on the fields, for they are white; already to harvest."*
>
> *John 4:35b*

He was giving them a faith picture of the spiritual harvest available for reaping. This was hope. With hope, faith has a framework on which to build. A concrete goal to aim for. Hope will anchor your mind on the promise of God. Hope will cause you to SEE yourself in possession of the promise. Like a builder who puts action to a blueprint plan by pouring the foundation and raising the walls, hope provides the plan for faith to act on. The devil wants you to keep your mind on the problems, challenges, struggles, high-costs, or anything negative that will keep your mind off the promise. But hope allows you to focus on what is possible with faith in God. Hope is vital to genuine faith.

What do you hope for? Get a promise from God's Word, and let your faith go after it. Use hope to SEE yourself in possession of that which was promised to you. You'll be surprised at how easily your faith will work when your hope is clear and definite.

Let's move on to other big enemies of faith and conquer them together.

■ **Enemy No. 6 — Considering the situation.**

> *"And being not weak in faith, he considered not his own body now dead, when he was about an hundred years old, neither yet the deadness of Sarah's womb."*

> Romans 4:19

Considering the situation instead of the promise of God is another enemy that robs us of the faith necessary for high performance living. To consider means "to ponder, observe, to keep before you, to meditate upon." Considering the situation, whatever it is, will make the situation grow instead of causing the solution to grow. Meditating upon the problem will always cause the problem to grow. Meditating on God's promises will cause faith to grow.

Do you remember the twelve spies Moses sent into the promised land to investigate? Two came back with a report based on God's promises. Ten returned with a report of the situation. Two fellows magnified the promise of God; ten magnified the problems of the situation. As it turned out, the two who focused on God's promise entered into the land and lived long and fruitful lives while the other ten died in the desert.

Some people believe only what they can see or feel. If they feel better, they believe they are better. Others believe what God's Word says regardless of how they feel. High performance believers consider God's promises rather than the situation. And they are winners. Always!

■ **Enemy No. 7 — Staggering at the promises.**

> *"He staggered not at the promise of God through unbelief; but was strong in faith, giving glory to God."*
>
> *Romans 4:20*

Here's another enemy of faith: staggering at the promises of God. This is the opposite of patient endurance. Remember, faith has steps. If you stagger up the steps, you'll fall. Staggering implies double-mindedness. You start out believing God for a specific promise, then you focus on the situation and begin to waver. Focusing on the situation drives out hope and destroys faith.

> *"But let him ask in faith, nothing wavering. For he that wavereth is like a wave of the sea driven with the wind and tossed."*
>
> *James 1:6*

A key to high performance living is to stay focused. Winners focus; losers spray. Staggering implies a loss of focus. When a camera is out of focus, it takes fuzzy pictures. When your faith is out of focus, you get fuzzy results.

When my son was very little, he said to me one day, "Hey daddy, wouldn't it be neat if you were a mailman?" I laughed, but it made me think about something. It made me think about focus. So often we are distracted by other possibilities. "Maybe I should take that part-time job as a realtor," we think to ourselves. This is especially tempting for ministers, who sometimes need some extra money. But these kinds of activities will cause us to lose focus on what we should be concentrating on.

> *"Let us hold fast the profession*
> *of our faith without wavering; (for*
> *He is faithful that promised.)"*
>
> *Hebrews 10:23*

Faith is a fight. But it's the best fight because faith always wins. Constantly affirm the promised outcome, even in the midst of contradictory evidence.

■ Enemy No. 8 — Not being fully persuaded.

> *"And being fully persuaded*
> *that, what He had promised, He was*
> *able also to perform."*
>
> *Romans 4:21*

Faith is the assurance of things hoped for. The only way I know how to be "fully persuaded" of this fact is to meditate on God's Word and talk with God in prayer *until* a sense of peace and confidence that I understand God's will floods my heart. Before we started construction on our multimillion dollar worship and teaching complex in Lansing, I got alone for days of prayer and Bible meditation. It wasn't until I had the assurance of God in my heart that we proceeded with the project. When you are fully persuaded, faith will carry you over any obstacle. When you are not, you will meet situations and challenges that will make you question your call or the legitimacy of your desired result.

Okay, let's review the enemies of faith we've covered in these last few chapters:

■ 1. Not understanding that faith is a process.

■ 2. Not having a specific promise from God.

■ 3. Not understanding the power of God.

■ 4. Unbelief or disbelief.

■ 5. Not understanding Bible hope.

■ 6. Considering the situation instead of the promises.

■ 7. Staggering at God's promise.

■ 8. Not being fully persuaded.

If you avoid these eight enemies, you'll be on your way to high performance faith living.

Chapter Seventeen
ADDITIVE #3: VIRTUE — ARETE
ACTIVE "INTERNAL EXCELLENCE" WORD
By Dick Mills

ARETE was a very active word in ancient Greece. The word has a non-biblical usage referred to by people who had an excellence about them. It described military heroes, owners of large estates, kings, and those of moral quality or great worth. ARETE was a favorite name for kings in Arabia and Asia Minor. As a proper name, it is found in 2 Corinthians 11:32, describing King Aretas who held sway over Damascus. In Greek thought, ARETE defined the virtue of a person as their beauty. The virtue of their physical body described their health and soundness. The virtue of their mind was described as goodness, truthfulness, or accuracy. The virtue of their disposition was described as generous, caring, giving, and bountiful liberality.

ARETE IN THE NEW TESTAMENT

ARETE (arr-ett-aye), Strong's #703, only appears five times in the New Testament. It is used to describe spiritual qualities that are the result of redemption. Some Bible scholars feel that the New Testament writers wanted to stay away from the idea that non-regenerated society, through self-help, could develop and improve on human nature without the aid of the Holy Spirit.

ARETE does have a lot of potential for the redeemed. If you believe that conversion to Christ is the starting place for a worthwhile and productive Christian life, then virtue (ARETE) has a big part to play in your growth and development.

Lexicons describe New Testament "virtue" (ARETE) as: "spiritual quality, extraordinary endowments, that which gives man his worth, his dignity, his efficiency, and his goodness."

Deissman found ARETE in the papyri references describing God's miracle power or manifestations of divine power. Some scholars believe ARETE came from "arsen" — the male, or from "airo" — to lift up, as a result of New Testament times, before women's liberation, when men did all the lifting of heavy objects. Therefore, "arsen" and "airo" declared that men were stronger for lifting. The ARETE person does not mind carrying his or her share of the load.

The ARETE person is an individual with "good stuff," "a role model," "an exemplary citizen," "a credit to his family," "one whose walk matched his talk" or as we would say "one whose lifestyle we admire and would do well to imitate." The hip crowd would call Mr. ARETE "a solid sender."

The bottom line on ARETE is "total masculinity without being macho, total femininity without being sensual." That quality of divine life imparted to a redeemed person that would not let them do anything less than their best for the Lord Jesus Christ.

"VIRTUE" TRANSLATIONS

New Century — *Goodness*

Amplified — *Excellence*

Beck — *Moral power*

Moffatt — *Resolution*

J.M. Ray — *Fortitude*

Young's — *Worthiness*

Doddridge — *Courage*

Godbey — *Heroism*

Montgomery — *Manliness*

Spencer — *Vigor*

Weymouth — *Noble character*

"Vital Christian life and growth
are a cooperative experience. God
does for us what we cannot do for
ourselves. But growth in grace de-
pends upon the believer (making
the effort)."
— Wesleyan Bible Commentary

Chapter Eighteen

VIRTUE

By Dave Williams

Someone said, "There are only two classes: first class and no class!"

In this chapter, you are going to discover the exciting ingredient to high performance living that will give you that "first class" quality in the eyes of others. They will observe your life and say, "Wow, that person has real class." What is this first class characteristic that draws the attention of others? Virtue!

Virtue is the ingredient that soups-up your performance ratings with high octane fuel. Virtue brings soundness to your body and goodness to your mind. Virtue brightens your disposition and brings dignity to your reputation. Its presence will show, unmistakably, in every aspect of your life.

You've known people who light up a room. Everybody is drawn to these people. There is a brightness and magnetism that radiates from them. The atmosphere changes when these folks walk in. They have a certain grace that rivets our attention. They are called "first class." What is it about these people that attracts us? Are they boisterous or brash? Do they deliberately try to call attention to themselves? No! What we find so attractive about these people comes from within. Virtue is the additive that makes them special.

"Virtue" was a popular name for kings in Peter's time. All the kings in Arabia and Asia Minor longed to be called "Virtue." It was thought that virtue brought extraordinary endowments to a person's life, thus many kings named themselves "Virtue." It seemed that people who developed this quality of virtue possessed greater giftings, unusual magnetism, far-reaching influence, and tremendous power.

Those kings desired the honor and power that went hand-in-hand with virtue. How can you have honor and power in your life? You must add virtue.

THE FIVE PRONGS OF VIRTUE

I call this the "five-pronged additive" because there are actually five specific definitions in the Greek language for the word, virtue. The first four prongs consist of things that YOU must do. The fifth prong is what GOD does when you accomplish the first four. When you activate the first four prongs, God comes on the scene and gives you the fifth prong — POWER in these areas of life:

■ Soundness of body

■ Goodness of mind

■ Brightness of disposition

■ Dignity of reputation

Let's closely examine the five prongs of virtue.

Chapter Nineteen
ETHICS & EXCELLENCE
By Dave Williams

■ **Prong No. 1 — Ethics.** People who are consistently prompt, polite, courteous, thoughtful, and proper are always attractive. We are drawn to people like that.

Ethics involves a large span of thoughtful things: from table manners to simple politeness. It reaches into the realm of kindness to all human beings, regardless of their position or stature in life. The man who shows particular kindness to a waitress who is under stress is said to have virtue. The man who opens the door for his wife, the lady who tips the cab driver, the man who takes time to chat with the garbage collector are all displaying virtue.

Examples of ethics:

■ 1. The business man who refuses to slander his competitors.

■ 2. The new pastor who speaks well of his predecessor.

■ 3. The person who listens to others carefully, without interrupting.

■ 4. The man who makes a habit of promptness.

■ 5. The person who refuses to dodge blame for mistakes, who won't shift responsibility to someone else.

■ 6. The one who is consistently reliable.

■ 7. The person who never says, "I told you so."

■ 8. The person who rejoices over other people's achievements rather than belittling them.

■ 9. The man who thinks about other people's needs, dreams, and plans rather than just his own.

■ 10. The worker who does his job completely, correctly, and contributes to the well being of his company.

■ 11. The one who makes others feel important.

■ 12. The lady at the office who will not become involved with gossip.

■ 13. The boss who says, "I'm proud of you."

■ 14. The person who says "thank you" in a timely manner.

The list could go on, but I think you get the idea.

Examples of unethical practices are all too common. A leading evangelist conducted a crusade in the Midwest. When he gave the invitation for people to come forward to receive Christ, a strange thing happened. There were more counselors available than they originally anticipated. It turned out that members of a national cult went among the new converts, handing out literature and offering to counsel them. This is an example of bad ethics. They couldn't get their own converts, so they tried to lead astray those who had been converted to Christ.

On another occasion, members of the same cult visited our bookstore after church one Sunday. Later we discovered they had secretly stocked our shelves with their free literature. We found it and threw it out. They were unethical and apparently know nothing about virtue.

On still another occasion, a social action group came to our church and stuffed the hymnal racks with their offering envelopes. They had a good cause, but because of their unethical conduct, we were forced to ban them from the church.

Virtue is refined morality. Its first prong is ethics. It means doing things right. Do you want to be the kind of person who lights up a room? If so, be prompt, be courteous, be kind, be polite — be ethical. Add to your faith VIRTUE. But there are four more prongs to virtue which we need to look at.

■ **Prong No. 2 — Excellence.** The difference between "first class" and "no class" is an attitude for excellence — a mind set that will only be satisfied with quality.

I think all of us have purchased an inferior product at one time or another thinking, "This will save me a few bucks." Did it work out? No! The cheap paper plates were so flimsy, your potato salad and chicken wings made an unscheduled landing in the dirt. The cheap paint peeled in a year; and not only did you have to buy more, but you had to spend a precious summer Saturday repainting the deck. So much for sacrificing quality to save a little money!

Sticking with excellence will put you much further ahead in the long run. That's the second definition of virtue — excellence, a touch of quality.

People who practice excellence are the best kind of people to have around you. They always do the job right the first time. You know you can depend on them. I like doing business with that kind of person. I don't like doing business with people who lack the virtue called excellence. I had a graphic example of the practical effect of excellence one weekend in St. Louis.

I missed my plane to Lansing. I ran to the counter and said, "Is that my plane taking off that I see through the window?"

"Yes, it is, Mr. Williams," the agent replied.

"Do you have another plane going to Lansing to-night?" I asked.

"No. Not until tomorrow," he said.

I ran from one airline agent to the next. No one had a flight to Lansing leaving that night! I had no choice but to arrange to spend the night in St. Louis.

I went to get a rental car. Nobody was standing in line at a well-known discount rental agency, so I thought, "Great, no waiting!" I never stopped to think there was probably a *reason* nobody else was interested in renting from this place.

"I've got to have a car tonight. Give me the cheapest one you've got," I said.

"We've only got one left, and it will be $57," he said. Well, I had to have a car, so I took it. That was at 5:00 PM on Friday. From my motel room, I made arrangements for a flight the next morning at 10:00 AM.

By Saturday morning at 9:00 AM, I had the car back to the rental agency. The tank was topped off, my keys turned in, my credit card billed. Everything was in order.

Two days later, the receipt arrived. I was charged for *two full days* of rental on a car I didn't even have for 24 hours. This place didn't have an 800 customer service number, so I called long distance. "Oh, I'm sorry, but I can't help you. You're going to have to call the guys at this number," they said.

I called the other number and finally got somebody to listen to me. The service representative acted like I was lying about having the car for only 16 hours, but after a lengthy discussion, he finally agreed to correct my bill and take the added charges off my credit card. When the next credit card bill came — you guessed it — no correction had been made. After this experience, I vowed never again to use this low-budget car rental business again.

Now I use a first class car rental agency that puts the principle of excellence to work. Whenever I go there, they roll out the red carpet.

I hand them my preferred customer card, and they say, "Oh, Mr. Williams, come right over to this little machine. I'll show you how it works, and then you won't ever have to wait in line again. I know how important your time is, Mr. Williams. You just put your card in here. Look! It says, 'Hi, Mr. Williams. Welcome! Please pick the car model you would like. Pick the color. Extra insurance?'" And presto! Out drop the keys! "If you have any problems Mr. Williams, just give us a call. That will be $29!" I feel like a king. At this place, I'm first class. At the other place, I felt like no class at all. That's virtue in action.

The first prong of virtue is ethics. The second prong is a determination to strive for excellence, to give your best in all your dealings with others. The third prong of virtue is honesty.

Chapter Twenty

HONESTY, MORAL GOODNESS & POWER

By Dave Williams

■ **Prong No. 3 — Honesty.** I love people who are honest. People who are genuine and straightforward don't pretend to be something that they're not or take advantage of your weakness or ignorance. Honest people are trustworthy, and everyone is drawn to someone they know they can trust.

I was talking to an evangelist the other day about a problem that he had overcome. He had struggled with the problem of lust. He was a powerful, anointed preacher with a touch from God; but he was also human and had this problem. He sought deliverance, and with God's help, he received it!

He was speaking at a church and shared this experience with the congregation. After the service, the pastor's wife sat him down and chastised him for so frankly discussing his personal problems.

"Don't you ever tell this church anything that you have ever struggled with. We want our people to look up to ministers," she rebuked.

His response was, "That's the problem. We've got too many ministers who are setting themselves way up above other people. When a flaw manifests, or a fault shows up, it's a pretty long way to fall. If we can't be honest about our failings, how will people ever trust us?"

I'll tell you what. I'm a very imperfect pastor, but I love Jesus Christ. I have the anointing of God on my life. If God loves me, even as I am, then I don't see any point in pretending to the rest of the world that I'm something that I'm not. I am a pilgrim in this progress — right along with everyone else — on the way to heaven.

Another facet of honesty is not taking advantage of someone. While I was ministering in Africa away from my family, my wife's car broke down back home. She took the car to the dealership, and the mechanic probably thought, oh, her husband is in Africa — she doesn't know much about cars, then said, "That will be $1,700 to fix it, Mrs. Williams."

She was so upset! And so was I when I found out. It infuriated me to think that someone would be so low as to take advantage of her. When I arrived home we took the car to a different mechanic. Forty dollars later, the problem was cured. Do you think I will ever go back to the first dealership again? If that first mechanic had just practiced virtue through honesty, he would have saved himself a customer.

Virtue is a compound of ethics, excellence, honesty and next, moral goodness.

■ **Prong No. 4 — Moral goodness.** Everywhere you go today you receive messages of immorality. Television programs flagrantly portray violence, sex, lying, cheating, and every other manner of sin, as acceptable. Advertising uses blatant sexuality to sell their products. Magazines tout immoral lifestyles as the desirable norm. The squeeze to seduce us into moral collapse is on.

If you want to have the power that will make you first class instead of no class — a high performance believer on high octane fuel — then moral goodness must be added to your life.

Moral goodness is how you conduct yourself. I remember the men I worked with before I went into the ministry. They were constantly flashing "pinup" pictures at me. They enjoyed getting to me, and it bothered me. Who wouldn't be bothered? On one hand, being a man I was having hot flashes, and on the other hand, being a Christian I was outraged.

One day, one of those perverts stuck a pinup in front of my face and said, "Hey! What do you think of that, religious boy?"

Suddenly, the Lord gave me a word of wisdom. "Well, I don't know what you've got waiting at home for you," I said, "but why should I look at an inferior, substandard body like that, when I've got a first class, first rate, knockout waiting for me at home!" That was the last time they ever flashed one of those disgusting pictures at me!

The Bible tells us to flee from youthful lusts. We all have a choice in how we conduct ourselves. If we refuse to buckle under pressure, to do what we know is wrong, we are being moral, a very important part of virtue.

When we have added the four parts of virtue to our faith, God will add the fifth part. The fifth prong, the result of adding ethics, excellence, honesty, and moral goodness to our lives is power.

■ **Prong No. 5 — Power.** God is a first class God. And He wants His believers to be first class too. When we add virtue to our faith and flow in His will, He will give us power. Power in the form of soundness of body, goodness of mind, radiance of disposition, and dignity of reputation. It is His promise to us.

Many Christians today try to operate in the gifts of the Spirit without ever seeking first to grow in the fruit of the Spirit. They say, "I'm seeking prophecy because I am a prophet." But if they sought to develop virtue in their lives, they would soon find that flowing in the spiritual gifts would come easily to them. God would give them that power.

Virtue. If you want to be a first class, high performance Christian, you will be diligent in developing the additive of virtue to your life. As you do, you will see that God will do His part by adding His power.

Chapter Twenty-One

ADDITIVE #4: KNOWLEDGE—GNOSIS

"HAVING THE FACTS" WORD

By Dick Mills

There are two main Greek words for "knowledge:" OIDA and GNOSIS (gno-sis). OIDA is a perceptive knowledge while GNOSIS is an acquired knowledge. When the Bible says that Jesus knew their thoughts, Luke 11:17, it was the EIDO/OIDA based word. He perceived, or could see, what they were thinking. The Latin word for OIDA is "video" or acquiring knowledge by sight. GNOSIS is essentially similar to "audio": acquiring knowledge by what you hear.

The word for "knowledge" in 2 Peter is GNOSIS, Strong's #1108. GNOSIS is used 29 times in the New Testament. Jesus called GNOSIS a key to knowing and understanding the heart of God. Generally GNOSIS signifies intelligence, understanding, having the facts, insights, awareness, Christian enlightenment, personal acquaintance, familiarity, recognition, enquiry, and seeking to know.

The New Testament usage of GNOSIS is related to general knowledge of: God, such as we find in the Gospels; Christ as we know our Savior; and what we know about spiritual truths and human responsibilities.

GNOSIS is a knowledge grounded on personal experience. A related word "ginosko" is used in Jesus' declaration, "You shall know (ginosko) the truth and the truth shall make you free," (John 8:32). Later when he told them, "I am the way the truth and the life," (John 14:6) we can readily see that knowing the truth is knowing Jesus.

GNOSIS is a knowledge that has inception, a starting place, a progress, a development, and a growth potential. When scripture states that knowledge shall be increased (Daniel 13:4), it assures us that walking with the Lord is a learning process. We never really quit developing as believers. Pastors are constantly urging believers to continue on in the growth process.

It is a joy to serve the Lord and discover new things about our Savior. GNOSIS frequently implies an active relationship between the one who "knows" and the person or thing "known." In 2 Peter 1:5, it says to add to your virtue knowledge. It is the open invitation to have an intimate acquaintance with our Lord that gives us a knowing awareness of how awesome our salvation really is.

"KNOWLEDGE"

TRANSLATIONS

Amplified — *Intelligence*

Jerusalem — *Understanding*

Knox — *Enlightenment*

New American — *Discernment*

A. Cressman — *Try to learn more*

Wuest — *Experiential knowledge*

Jordan — *Wisdom*

Ledyard — *A better understanding*

"Gnosis gives us a more complete and profound acquaintance
with the Lord. He acts in our heart
and helps us in our walk. We become more humble, more sober
minded. We know better where
our treasure is and what it is. This
is the true knowledge of God."
                              —J.N. Darby

Chapter Twenty-Two

KNOWLEDGE

By Dave Williams

*"And beside this, giving all dili-
gence, add to your faith virtue; and
to virtue knowledge."*

2 Peter 1:5

Faith is the foundation of our spiritual life. Virtue gives
our spiritual life moral direction. Knowledge is the additive that we apply to keep our spiritual life growing. Do
you want to be a high performance believer? Then you need
to use every gift God has given to you. He gave you the gift
of a brain — learn how to use it well!

If we don't apply active intelligence to our faith, then
we are easy prey to every new doctrinal wind that blows.
Isaiah 5 tells us that people actually come into captivity and
bondage due to a lack of knowledge. "Therefore my people

are gone into captivity, because they have no knowledge: and their honorable men are famished, and their multitude dried up with thirst." (See Isaiah 5:13.) Without a foundation of knowledge, without a fundamental and deep rooted understanding of God's will as revealed to us in the Bible, we are easy victims of every smooth-talking, silver-tongued huckster that Satan sends our way.

It is vital that we perfect our knowledge of God (theology) and our knowledge of His son, Jesus Christ (Christology). Wrongly held beliefs at the foundation of our faith will destroy the entire structure of our spiritual lives, leaving us in ruin. If you get on the wrong road from the very beginning, you will never arrive at the right destination — no matter how long you keep chugging on.

Have you ever known someone who tried to operate in the gifts of the Spirit but had no scriptural knowledge on how to do so intelligently? I have known people like this. There was a person, who liked to be recognized as a prophet, who stood and proclaimed, "Thus saith the Lord, fear not my children. But don't worry if you do fear because sometimes I'm afraid Myself, saith the Lord." A thorough knowledge of God, through the study of His Word, is absolutely necessary for successfully flowing in spiritual gifts.

So, how do we gain the knowledge we need so we don't go chugging down the wrong road?

Proverbs 1:7 says this, "The fear of the Lord is the beginning of knowledge...." Here, the word fear means respect — reverence for God and His Word. When we are filled with respect and reverence, then we are at the starting place for obtaining true knowledge. A person who says, "I don't believe that Jesus Christ was the Son of God, he was just a really great teacher, like Mohammed or Confucius," shows that he has not even found the starting point of knowledge. The beginning place of knowledge is fear of the Lord.

Proverbs 1:7 goes on to say, "But fools despise wisdom and instruction." Do you want to be a fool? Then despise learning. Do you think God wants you to be kept in the dark about His will? Look at Proverbs 1:22, "How long, ye simple ones, will ye love simplicity? And the scorners delight in their scorning, and fools hate knowledge?" I wonder how anti-intellectual Christians would explain this verse. It is clear to me that God doesn't have much patience with people who choose to remain ignorant.

If the unfortunate people who are drawn into these modern, destructive cults would just make the effort to seek enlightenment from God for themselves, their lives and eternal souls would never be at jeopardy. Each time a believer needs a prophetic word, he doesn't have to rush to some person but can go directly to the source, God's Word. Through the Holy Ghost, the enlightenment he needs is available.

I am not going to debate Mary Baker Eddy's writings, or Charles Taze Russell's writings, or the writings of some of the more contemporary cultists. People who believe and follow these doctrines have their minds set.

Once I was ministering at a funeral, and a lady approached me. "Oh, that was such a good message you gave, Pastor Williams. It was wonderful. By the way, in what manner do you baptize at your church?"

I responded, "Well, you know, we cover all the bases. We baptize in the name of God the Father, Jesus Christ the Son, and God the Holy Spirit. Therefore, we baptize in the name of the Father, Son, and Holy Ghost and in the Name of Jesus Christ."

"Hmm," she said, "but do you say 'in the name of Jesus' when they go under, or do you say 'in the name of the Father, Son, and Holy Ghost,' when they go under?"

People get so caught up in all these little side trips! The important thing is that when they baptized me, or anyone else, we went under that water, leaving our old life behind.

> *"For that they hated knowledge, and did not choose the fear of the Lord: They would none of my counsel: they despised all my reproof."*
>
> *Proverbs 1:29-30*

Another sad result of failing to seek knowledge is seen in Proverbs 1:31-32.

"Therefore shall they eat of the fruit of their own way, and be filled with their own devices. For the turning away of the simple shall slay them, and the prosperity of fools shall destroy them."

God is saying, "They didn't ask My counsel. They despised My reproof. Therefore, they shall have to suffer the consequences. They wanted to do things their own way, now they must accept the results." God will let us make the mistakes we choose to make, and He will let us live with the results.

It is not spiritual to refuse to use your brain. When you do, you leave yourself open to destructive forces. However, as in anything, it is possible to go to extremes. There are two extremes in the attitudes of Christians toward knowledge.

The first extreme is the false belief that knowledge is god. This is really the worship of Baal, or the worship of the intellect. This kind of Christian places all his confidence in human knowledge. He thinks if you have one or two Ph.D.'s, then every word you say must be truly inspired of God.

The danger lurks in thinking that mere education is an indicator of spirituality. Human knowledge is so limited. Human knowledge will tell us that $2 + 2 = 4$, but human knowledge will never tell us what the need of someone's heart is. Only God's knowledge, revealed supernaturally, can give us that.

The opposite extreme is believing that knowledge is nothing. The anti-intellectual Christian will say, "Man, I'll tell you what! I'm just like the old disciples. I came off the fishing boat, and I don't need any education." It's funny how this kind of Christian never stops to think that Jesus spent a great deal of His time teaching His disciples! He felt their education was pretty important.

Anti-intellectuals are opposed to rational thinking, and many will try to pass it off as great faith. Have you ever heard of somebody who quit taking their insulin by faith and then died? I read about a young boy who died because his parents wouldn't give him medical help when his appendix burst. They wouldn't take him to the doctor because they had "faith." The boy died because of their ignorance. Do you think God is stupid? God can heal you even if you are on medication. It's not faith to throw away something that's keeping you alive.

My wife used to wear glasses. She knew the moment she was healed. She laid her glasses on the altar and knew that God had healed her eyes — she's never worn glasses since. But if she had walked away from that altar stumbling, she could have gone back, picked up her glasses, and said, "Maybe next time, Lord." That would have been the reasonable, intelligent thing to do.

"Knowing I know not" is a big step on the road to knowledge. But how do Christians learn what they need to know to have a successful Christian walk? In the next chapter are some good directions to the path of learning.

Chapter Twenty-Three
FINDING KNOWLEDGE
By Dave Williams

I think Christians should be the smartest, most intelligent, intellectual people in the world. This can be done without being a dull, boring snob too. One of the most entertaining times I have ever experienced was at a breakfast with Dr. Glen Cole, a pastor and executive national presbyter, and Dr. Peter Kho, a successful medical doctor. These guys were smart and very well educated. Their conversation was challenging yet humorous, light yet absorbing. I know that Satan would have a very hard time deceiving these men with his lies!

Without education, we have no objective defense against heresy and damnable doctrines. In Galatia, after Paul's successful crusade where hundreds came to Jesus Christ, the converts did not grow in their knowledge of spiritual truth, thus they became vulnerable and were led astray. They were brought into bondage, enslaved by heresy, losing the joy they had found in knowing Jesus.

Knowledge will protect us from damaging doctrines and hucksters who would lead us astray. Knowledge will lead us to a deeper and more intimate understanding of God and His will. It is an important additive for high octane faith. What are the best sources for obtaining knowledge?

■ **1. The Bible.** When I was in flight school, one of the first things I learned was that hot air doesn't give you as much lift as cold air. So, on real hot days, you have to allow extra room on the runway for a successful takeoff. That information was right there in my flight manual.

One day, a pilot decided to take his plane out. It was a hot day, and he came to the point on the runway where he needed to lift off. He got a couple of feet off the ground and SMASH... he slammed into a tree. As he stumbled from the wreckage, his first words were, "Oh, wow! I wonder what happened!" Well, he forgot to consult his flight manual. He didn't know the rules, and that got him into trouble.

The Bible is a Christian's flight manual. It contains all the information you need to walk successfully with the Lord. But unless you study the Bible, planting its precepts firmly in your heart and mind, you will end up like that guy in the plane...in for a crash landing.

■ **2. Other good books.** Find and study good books that are written by people who are strongly founded in biblical principles. Christian book stores are filled with books written by people who want to help you become the best you can be. If you want to be a high octane believer, reach out for the help you can find in good books.

■ **3. A Bible training institute.** Find a good school, one that is teaching proven Christian principles; then take some classes. You will be amazed at how anointed teachers can fuel the flame of faith.

■ **4. Listen to anointed preaching.** It has never been so easy to have access to inspired preaching. Of course the preaching you hear on Sunday is great, but additionally, most of the world's best preachers have audio and video tapes available to you. Anytime you want, you can be inspired by a great preacher — and as you listen, take notes! You will understand and remember 75% more because you will really be concentrating on what is said.

■ **5. Converse with believers.** Join a Bible study group or a Christian social group, and take the opportunity to discuss what you have learned with others. It is a great chance to practice what you learn on Sunday morning.

■ **6. Personal meditation.** Facts alone can't bring about change in your life. You can come to church, hear the truth, write it down — but nothing inside you will be changed until it really sinks into your soul. If you put food into your mouth, chewed it up, and then spat it out, your body wouldn't receive any nourishment.

Spiritual food is the same way. Your spirit won't be nourished until you take what you learn and digest it. Meditation is the process we use to digest the Word.

How do you meditate on the Word? Take a portion of the Bible — for example, Psalm 1. Read it every chance you get. Memorize it. Read it to someone else, and ask them what they think it means. Think about that Psalm continually; examine it from every angle. Speak it. Mutter it over and over. Eventually the truth of Psalm 1 is going to melt down into your spirit and feed you. You will feel something inside. That is when you know that the Word is really becoming a part of your life.

The closer you draw to the Lord through the knowledge of His Word, the more power and vitality you will experience in your life. When everyone else is complaining of low octane faith, you will be burning hot on the high-octane fuel that KNOWLEDGE has added to your faith.

Chapter Twenty-Four

ADDITIVE #5: SELF-CONTROL — EGKRATEIA

"KEEPING YOUR COOL" WORD

By Dick Mills

The two opposite self words are self-gratification and self-control. One wise man walked on a university campus with an archway that read "Know Yourself." He suggested they rewrite the slogan to "Behave Yourself." Out of the nine additives, self-control is one that is behavioral in scope and is notably connected with vibrant Spirit-filled living. Galatians 5:16 succinctly states, "Walk in the Spirit and you shall not fulfill the lust of the flesh."

The Greek word for self-control is "EGKRATEIA" (eng-krat'-i'ah), Strong's #1466, and it appears four times in the Greek New Testament. Earlier the King James writers (1611 AD) had translated the word as temperance. Over time, the word temperance came to mean a pledge to abstain from alcoholic beverages. EGKRATEIA was a much larger word, though it included abstinence from tobacco, drugs, and alcoholic drinking.

The more recent translations including the New King James, wisely expanded the "temperance" translation to include the whole range of "self-control."

EGKRATEIA is a compounded word made up of "eg" — within, and "kratos" — strength or power. The resident Holy Spirit who dwells in our temples of clay permanently gives the power to overcome the flesh, the world, and the devil (James 3:15). Eric Liddell, in Chariots of Fire said, "The power is within."

Some lexical definitions of EGKRATEIA are, "self-mastery," "command over the appetites," "the grace by which the fleshly inclinations are controlled," "self-restraint," "power over one's desires," "moderation," "dominion one has over himself," "self-government," "to hold oneself in," "to command oneself," "to say 'no' to one's body," "having a firm grip on oneself," and "being in control of your emotions."

John Wesley defined EGKRATEIA as "voluntarily abstaining from any pleasure which does not lead us to God."

"TEMPERANCE"

TRANSLATIONS

Barclay — *Self mastery*

A. Cressman — *Try to make yourself do what is right*

Douay — *Abstinence*

Fenton — *Self-restraint*

Godbey — *Holiness*

Hammond — *Strict continence*

Knox — *Continence*

Living Bible — *To put aside your own desires*

Ledyard — *Able to say no when you need to*

Shuttleworth — *The restraint of our passions*

"A man may eat too much bread. He may drink too much water. He may surfeit himself with too much food. He may go too far even in legitimate directions, and having gone too far he has gained no advantage. He has actually lost the advantage with which he started. Moderation is enjoyment. Being temperate is the true delight. Self-control is real power."

—Joseph Parker

Chapter Twenty-Five
TEMPERANCE
By Dave Williams

*"And to knowledge temperance;
and to temperance patience; and to
patience godliness."*

2 Peter 1:6

We have discussed diligence, faith, virtue, knowledge, and now, the next additive for high performance living — temperance.

What do you think of when you hear the word temperance? Does the picture of a bunch of crabby old ladies carrying signs and playing tambourines as they march down the road to break up a tavern with axes come to mind? Or does it mean abstaining from drinking, smoking, swearing, or chewing tobacco? To some it may mean keeping your temper.

Temperance means self-control which leads to emotional stability. The opposite of temperance is what Paul promised would be the indicator of end times: incontinence (2 Timothy 3). No, that doesn't mean poor bladder control! It means unstable emotions, spinning out of emotional control. Someone who is intemperate is the prey of addictions and displays inappropriate behavior.

Anything that is out of control is sick. If the cells of your body grow out of control, you have cancer. If the members of a society are out of control, that society is sick. If a government is out of control, it is a sick government. If a person is unable to control his actions or attitudes, that is a sick person.

We all know of stories where cars have gone out of control and wrought horrible damage. We remember when the fires in California raged out of control devouring everything in their path. But there's something far more dangerous and tragic when it gets out of control than a fire or an automobile, and that's a human life that's out of control.

The human tongue, human addictions, and human emotions, when out of control, are all more deadly and dangerous than a raging fire. They can do far more damage to society. Temperance is the opposite of erratic, unstable, addictive behavior. People who have added temperance to their lives know where they are going, and they know how to get there within the boundaries of God's grace.

Electricity is one of man's greatest servants. Properly harnessed, it provides light and heat for our homes, it cooks our food, it makes it possible for us to travel, talk on the phone — it gives us so many blessings. But unharnessed, it is a horrible, destructive force. Lightning bolts can rend trees in half, sometimes even kill people. Downed electrical wires are a dangerous hazard.

A river, flowing between its banks, is a blessing. Commerce travels on it, people swim and boat on it. But if it breaks through its banks, it can destroy whole towns. Without banks, you don't have a river, you have a swamp. People who lose control of their lives are like a swamp, not a mighty river with direction and purpose.

What would it be like if we didn't have any highways or roads? What if there were no guides or boundaries so that we never knew exactly where we were going, or even the direction from which we came? If you wanted to go to another town, you would just set out in the general direction and stumble around until you found it. Or, you would have to carry a lot of navigational equipment that would tell you if you were on the right path.

That is what life would be like without rules and guidelines and a sense of self-discipline. The root of the word temperance is "strength." Temperance — self-control — makes us strong.

Unfortunately, many lives are out of control today. Drinking, spending money, smoking, drugs, sex, food, and violence are just some of the ways that people get themselves into bondage. People always have excuses. "I'm not fat; I'm just big boned." "I don't drink too much. I can quit anytime I want; I just don't want to." "I have so much stress in my life, I just take these pills to take the edge off; I'm not addicted though — I can quit anytime." Unfortunately all the excuses in the world won't change the facts: they have lost control of some aspect of their lives, and they are now being controlled by their weakness.

Many would much rather control others than themselves. I would rather control the way you think and your emotions and how you treat me, than I would to control myself and my reaction to the way I've been treated. But temperance is SELF-control, not control of others.

Solomon said the man (or woman) who lacks self-control is like a city that is broken down, whose walls are no longer there. In other words, lack of self-control — lack of temperance — will break your life down, and the walls of protection will no longer be there. The Bible says the fruit of the Spirit is love, joy, peace, and temperance — self-control.

For years we have sent leaders to Washington who do not apply temperance to the job of leading this country. As a result, the national spending deficit is staggering.

Even if our government stopped overspending today, it would take decades to pay off this huge debt. Cheating, dishonesty, and greed are apparent even in some of our nation's leaders.

The Social Security System is out of control. When it began back in 1937, it seemed like a good idea. It would provide a secure retirement for everyone. But in the 1950's and 1960's, the government began to borrow from this huge fund. They raided the funds, leaving a bad IOU and potential bankruptcy in its wake. What a system! It's out of control because of intemperance and incontinence. We are living in the day which Paul spoke about when men would be lovers of their own selves, covetous, boasters, high-minded traitors, disobedient, ungrateful wretches that are totally out of control.

We are living in an out-of-control society, and we need believers — people who have submitted to the Lordship of Jesus Christ — to rise up and say, "I'm going to be temperate and self-controlled and purposeful. I am going to be led by a sense of mission. I am going to make something of myself." The Holy Spirit wants to be a co-laborer in our efforts. He wants to be on our team, beside us all the way, shoulder to shoulder.

Temperance means controlling your tongue as well. James said the man who cannot bridle his tongue has a vain religion, or an empty, dead religion that does him no good. I was talking to one of my daughter's friends. She told me that her mother said we "brainwash" people at Mount Hope Church. I responded, "We try to clean up minds at Mount Hope Church, but we never try to control anyone. People may come and go as they like. We don't force everyone to look alike or to do exactly the same things. We just try to show everyone the truth of God's Word." Don't speak rumors without any facts. It shows a lack of self-control.

Chapter Twenty-Six

WHAT IS SELF-CONTROL?

By Dave Williams

Nobody wants to be on the highway when a car goes out of control or in a building with a raging fire. A person who is out of control can hurt anyone he meets.

We live in times when there is great economic, political, social, and financial instability. We live in times when all the tried and true moral precepts seem to have been thrown out the window. ABC's Ted Koppel put it best, "Ladies and Gentlemen, the Ten Commandments are not the ten suggestions!"

God gave us curbs, river banks, roads, and boundaries. We have our instructions. If we want to be high performance believers, we need to follow them. We need to exercise self-control. How do we do it?

■ **1. Understand that self-control is not self-discipline.** Self-discipline is "I must stay on the road. I must do this. I must do that. I am going to force myself with every ounce of my energy to do what I'm supposed to do." You might be able to make it this way, but odds are, you won't. The flesh is weak. This was the Pharisees' mistake. They thought by having lots of rules and following them perfectly, they would become perfect. But that is pure misery for most people. Self-control is different; it is a fruit of the Spirit. When you find yourself starting to get out of control, you can say, "Holy Spirit, because Jesus is living in my life, You are living in my life. The fruit of Your presence is temperance. Therefore, Holy Spirit, let that self-control take over."

I do it, and I know it works. It's a miracle when you stop the grueling self-discipline and instead let the Holy Spirit develop self-control in your life. Then it becomes a joy! You are not some drone Christian, struggling under your heavy burdens. With self-control, it's not a struggle; it's a gift!

■ **2. If there is an area of abuse or intemperance in your life, recognize it and admit it.** Confess it before God. Don't try to shift the blame or responsibility. Own up to it, and then God will be able to help you.

There was a man who drank a case of beer every day. He denied that he had a drinking problem, but he just kept getting sicker and sicker. He determined it was because he drank too many fluids, so he switched to scotch and water. When he continued to get sicker, he decided it must be the water, so he gave that up!

The blood of Jesus cleanses confessed sin. So confess it. "Lord, I have this drinking problem. I am out of control. I can't make it without your help."

■ **3. Run to God for help; run to Jesus for help.** Do you know why? The devil will work to wear down your will and get you to do something that pulls your life out of control. Then he will tell you, "There, you've blown it now. You've broken God's heart. He doesn't want anything to do with you now." The devil will put that in your mind until you think God is the enemy. Pretty soon you and God aren't talking anymore; the line of communication has been cut.

Remember this. God knows every terrible thing that you are capable of. He knows you can blow it. He doesn't care; He loves you anyway. You can never sink so low that you will escape God's care and love for you. Isn't that wonderful!

What a miracle! God loves us even though He knows us and our faults. That means that no matter what, we are safe with God. Others may try to beat us into submission and bend us to their will, but with God we are safe. Just go to Him, and lay it all out. You will be happy and relieved when you do.

■ **4. Avoid whatever it is in your life that tempts you to lose control.** If you are addicted to food, stop eating for a day. If you are addicted to shopping, stop shopping for a week. Stop the addictive behavior NOW.

A young man wanted to be wise. So he went to a wise man and asked, "How do I obtain wisdom?" The wise man took the youth to a cave and put him in there with a truckload of books and said, "Stay in here until you have gotten wise." Before he left, the old man took out a bag of itching powder and sprinkled some into the student's hands.

The next day the wise man came back and asked the youth if he had grown wise. The boy said, "I haven't even finished one of these books, I spend most of my time scratching!" The old man nodded, sprinkled some more powder into the boy's hands, and left.

Day after day this went on. The boy couldn't make any progress in reading the books because he was tormented by the itching in his hands. Finally, one day the old man came back and went to sprinkle the dust in the boy's hands again. The lad snatched away the bag and threw it in the fire.

"Ah," said the old man. "At last you have learned wisdom. You may leave this cave now. You are wise. You have finally learned that wisdom is more than knowledge from a book. It is learning that you can make a choice."

That, my friend, is being in control. If there is something itching you in your life, you can do something about it. The Holy Spirit will give you self-control. Practice temperance in your life, and experience the joy that freedom from controlling addictions can bring you.

Chapter Twenty-Seven
ADDITIVE #6: PERSEVERANCE —
HUPOMONE

THE "ENDURING" WORD
By Dick Mills

Sandwiched between self-control and godliness is a word that shows us how to endure. HUPOMONE is the word associated with "staying power." We hear of people who are "sticking it out," "going the distance," "staying on course," and "in for the long haul." HUPOMONE has to do with a "marathon mentality," "a patient frame of mind," "standing your ground," or "holding out."

HUPOMONE (hoop-ohm-on-aye), Strong's #5281, is a durability word. A compound of "hupo" — to be under and "meno" — to abide or to remain. Early grammarians defined this compound word as "remaining behind, abiding under, or staying under. It is a steadfast endurance, a bearing up under, or consistency." HUPOMONE included fortitude, cheerful endurance, and persevering coura-geously in testing times because of one's confidence in God's faithfulness and power. An example is shown by David's declaration in Psalm 56:3, "Whenever I am afraid, I will trust in you."

There is also in patience an element of hope, confi-dence, trust, and looking to the future. HUPOMONE does not resign stoically to every day situations, and it does not sit down and give in to circumstances. A biblical per-spective of perseverance contains an active content with a forward look. Further, HUPOMONE does not complain about the darkness because of the knowledge of the com-ing dawn. Jesus endured the cross because He was able to see the joy that was set before Him (Hebrews 12:2).

HUPOMONE always carries hope. HUPOMONE says "weeping may endure for the night but joy is coming in the morning," (Psalm 30:5). "They that sow in tears shall reap in joy," (Psalm 126:5). "Many are the afflictions of the righteous but the Lord delivers him out of them all," (Psalm 34:19).

Michael Green said of HUPOMONE, "It's the temper of mind which is unmoved by difficulty or distress." Bible translators say of HUPOMONE, "It is the capacity to bear up under difficult circumstances." Thayer states that HUPOMONE is "the temperament which does not easily succumb when under pressure. It is the opposite of cow-ardice or despondency."

"PATIENCE"

TRANSLATIONS

King James — *Patience*

RSV — *Steadfastness*

Fenton — *Obedience*

Laubach — *Standing firm*

Ledyard — *Do not give up*

Septuagint — *Patient hope*

Basic English — *A quiet mind*

NEB — *Fortitude*

Schonfield — *Constancy*

C.B. Williams — *Patient endurance*

Weymouth — *Endurance*

"HUPOMONE is a root of all that is good. Fruit that never withers. A fortress that is never taken. A harbor that knows no storms. It is the Queen of Virtues, the Mother of Reverence, the Foundation of Right Actions. It is peace in war, calm in tempest, security in the midst of conspiracies. It is the quality which keeps a man on his feet with his face to the wind."
—John Chrysostrom

Chapter Twenty-Eight
THE IMPORTANCE OF PATIENCE
By Dave Williams

Try to imagine what life must have been like a few hundred years ago. There weren't any telephones. Sometimes people waited months or even years to receive a letter from a loved one. There weren't any fast food restaurants, jet airplanes, fax machines, or fast cars. The pace of living had to be slower. People didn't have any choice. You would have gotten some pretty strange looks if you asked for a cup of instant coffee or if you wanted to know where the nearest "ready-teller" could be found. Instant gratification was not an expectation people had concerning most things.

Now, people become violently angry if they are driving behind someone who is going five miles below the speed limit or if they have to stand in a checkout line at the grocery store for more than a minute. Why wait an hour for a baked potato when the microwave can give you one in six minutes? If asked, most people would say they have very little patience. It is not something most people are born with, but it can be developed. Peter thought patience was a vital quality for the Christian believer to develop.

> *"And to knowledge temperance;*
> *and to temperance patience; and to*
> *patience godliness..."*
>
> *2 Peter 1:6*

What is this quality called patience, and how can adding this quality to our lives help us become high performance believers?

A little boy was asked to define patience and responded, "It's when you sit in church and the preacher preaches and preaches, and you sit there, and sit there, and sit there." This may be a little unflattering to preachers, but in a certain way, it describes patience. The word patience actually means two things: waiting and enduring. The word endurance can be defined as a strong willed tenacity that never gives up, even in the face of poor odds.

Patience is a winning additive for every Christian. Once developed, patience will do six very important things in our lives.

■ **1. Patience will always promote us.** Shammah was one of King David's three top leaders. The only record we have of Shammah's deeds in service to the King was guarding his pea patch from the invading Philistines. All his compatriots deserted their posts but not Shammah. No matter what, he just stayed there in that patch guarding the peas, persevering in his humble task, fighting off every Philistine. His patience was rewarded by his promotion as one of the great men of his day.

God will reward us in the same way. If He plants you in a small ministry, or puts you in charge of a seemingly humble task, be patient. Hang in there. Stick to it. Wait and watch. Soon you will become one of God's great servants on earth.

■ **2. Patience will always strengthen us.**

> *"My brethren, count it all joy when ye fall into divers temptations; Knowing this, that the trying of your faith worketh patience. But let patience have her perfect work, that ye may be perfect and entire, wanting nothing."*
>
> *James 1:2-4*

There are people who have a tendency to uproot themselves continuously. It becomes a way of life as they restlessly wander from relationship to relationship, church to church. Whenever a problem crops up or things don't go exactly their own way, they're off! They never learn the patience to stick with a situation through the good times and bad, so they never develop spiritual strength. Patience strengthens you. Every high performance believer has come to realize the magnificent power of this additive.

Often people come to me and say, "Brother Dave, I've been going to such-and-such a church for two years, but I'm just not being fed over there anymore." I never open my arms and welcome them right in. I tell them to go back and earnestly pray for their church and for their pastor and then stay put.

If you keep uprooting a plant and transplanting it from place to place, the plant will never thrive. It will be stunted and sickly, and eventually it may even die. People are much the same way. If they uproot and transplant themselves from church to church, they will never allow themselves the chance to develop the deep, strong roots of faith that go all the way down to living waters. When I look out at my congregation, I see the faces of people who have been planted and strongly growing in the church for many years. I know that they will always bear fruit. Their roots are down deep, far below the momentary trials and troubles that wither others who have never stayed in one place long enough to patiently develop the deep roots of faith.

There will always be problems. Things will never go the way you want them to 100 percent of the time. But patient endurance will build your strength to see those bad times through to victory.

■ **3. Patience will always provide a bridge to receiving the promises of God.**

> *"That ye be not slothful, but followers of them who through faith and patience inherit the promises. For when God made promise to Abraham, because he could swear by no greater, he sware by Himself, Saying, Surely blessing I will bless thee, and multiplying I will multiply thee. And so, after he had patiently endured, he obtained the promise."*
>
> Hebrews 6:12-15

When we have faith, we begin to believe the promises we find in the Bible. When we couple our faith with patience, we build a supernatural bridge up to the time where we receive those promises. Faith comes; we believe. Patience then builds the bridge we walk until we receive the blessings that God has promised us.

But what do some people do? They start out strong, believing God for a promise. Then they begin to waver. They look around, and the promise just doesn't seem to be happening. They wait a little while, but still there is no delivery on the promise. So, that's it! They quit believing. They don't apply patient endurance to the situation, so the promise is never fulfilled to them. It's tragic to think that maybe in just a few more days, or even hours, they would have seen God's hand moving in their lives. They just didn't stand in faith and wait.

On the other hand, there are some who have developed patience as a key ingredient to their faith. They take hold of a promise and just keep walking the bridge of patience until it comes. They refuse to get off that bridge; they can't be budged or swayed. They won't speak a word against that promise; they just keep speaking, and believing, and patiently waiting until God delivers.

Remember Daniel's prayer? He prayed for 21 days. He just wouldn't let go until his answer came. Then an angel of the Lord arrived. In essence he said, "Daniel, it's a good thing you prayed and didn't give up. The first day you prayed, God released the answer from heaven, and I was sent to bring it to you. But on my way, I ran into some forces of darkness. My armies and I had to fight against them until we won. It was a good thing you kept praying, Daniel, because your faith helped us conquer those forces of spiritual darkness and deliver the answer to you."

Now suppose Daniel had prayed 20 days and then said, "That's it! I guess God isn't going to send me an answer, so forget it!" His answer might have been even longer delayed. Patience will provide the bridge for us to walk until we receive our answered promise from God.

So if you need healing in your body or relief from financial burdens — whatever your need might be — find God's promise as it relates to your situation, then stand on it. Don't ever give up or let go. Focus your patience on the situation and never doubt that God will keep His word to you!

■ **4. Patience will always result in happiness.**

> *"Behold, we count them happy which endure. Ye have heard of the patience of Job, and have seen the end of the Lord; that the Lord is very pitiful, and of tender mercy."*
>
> *James 5:11*

■ **5. Patience will always build character.** On judgement day, we will not be judged by the way we were able to use our charisma to sway crowds or our personal magnetism to lead people to church. We will be judged by the character we have developed in this life and by how much like Jesus we became. Patience will build our character.

My wife, Mary Jo, has learned patience in her life through her experiences with our little dog, Cashew. Our daughter, Trina, was born with a natural love for anything that moved. From bugs to birds, she has always been a creature lover. We feel it is a beautiful quality and never tried to discourage her in it, but Mary Jo just does not share the same appreciation. She thinks animals are fine, as long as they are outside.

Trina had real faith, though. The Bible says if you have faith as a grain of mustard seed, you can move mountains, and Trina had it. When she was still a very little girl, she saved up her money and bought a leash. That was her first step of faith. We just told her to keep on believing, and eventually her faith increased — and we ended up with a cockapoo.

That's when Mary Jo's trial of endurance really began. Of course, as a tiny puppy, Cashew made her little messes about the house. We expected them, and really she was so adorable, and we were so in love with her, that it wasn't hard to put up with. But for some reason, the little messes never seemed to stop. As the months wore on, Mary Jo found it more and more difficult to tolerate. She is a wonderful housekeeper, and it is very important to her to have a clean, orderly house — she works very hard at it. Even though Trina was very faithful in cleaning up after Cashew, it became harder and harder for Mary Jo to love our messy little dog.

We took Cashew to the vet, and there was nothing physically wrong; she just had a problem controlling her elimination. Many times Mary Jo would talk about finding a new home for Cashew, but there was something so absolutely loving about that little dog that we just couldn't do it. No matter how bad she messed up, she always greeted us with such utter adoration. When punished, she never held a grudge. It was so obvious she wanted to be good and please us, but time after time she failed.

Finally, Trina said to her mother, "Mom, I think you're trying to give this problem to God, but then you take it right back. You aren't giving God a chance to solve the problem."

Well, Mary Jo really wanted to overcome this situation, and though she didn't have any faith in Cashew, she did have faith in God. She believed that God cared about her and did not want her to be unhappy. So, she began to continually put this problem in His hands. After awhile, she began to notice that the messes just didn't bother her as much, and gradually Cashew began to do better.

Today, if you ask Mary Jo what lesson Cashew has taught her, she will tell you that our little dog has taught her patience. She says, "I just think of how many times I wanted to give up on Cashew. But now a prayer I pray quite often is, 'God I just want to be so good, and many times I fail. God, just don't give up on me.'"

It seems to us that Cashew was put in our lives to teach us about not giving up and being patient. It is a character trait that is good for every believer to build upon.

■ **6. Patience will always take us closer to the exponential curve for miracles.**

What do I mean by exponential curve? This is most easily seen in compounded interest. A young man starts faithfully putting $10 a week in a savings account. That's just $520 a year, not much at all. But patiently, faithfully, he persists. Year after year, he invests his money in an interest bearing account. For a long time, the money grows very slowly, but finally there is a point where that money reaches an exponential curve; and the interest, compounding on the interest, begins to accrue quickly. Almost overnight the fund skyrockets. The seemingly insignificant yearly amount, compounding interest, becomes a million or more!

So many people never understand the potential of exponential growth. They gratify themselves today and refuse to patiently wait for the miracle of exponential growth.

I know of a pastor who never made more than $12,000 a year in his whole life. In fact, that was the most he ever made in one year of his whole ministry. He retired at the age of 62, and because of his faithful program of investment, he retired as a millionaire!

That kind of patience can bring you closer to God's exponential curve of miracles. The more faith you invest, with patience, in God's promises, the more God will reward you with the fulfillment of His promises in your life. Soon you will see your small, daily, faith investments returning to you magnified by the loving generosity of our Heavenly Father.

Patience is a very important additive for the high performance Christian to add to his faith. In the next chapter, we will share some simple strategies to develop this trait in your life.

Chapter Twenty-Nine
STRATEGIES FOR BUILDING PATIENCE
By Dave Williams

As we discussed in the previous chapter, patience is a vital additive for every Christian who wants to walk in victory; who wants to live a life that will be a testimony to the power of walking with Jesus.

Patience is composed of two elements: forbearance, or a willingness to wait on the Lord; and endurance, which is a gritty tenacity that will not give up or doubt the promises of God. Endurance won't let go no matter how things look, or how bad the odds may seem, or how much the circumstances may appear to be against the promises. The successful believer, who has developed these two qualities, will always know an inner peace.

How do we develop these qualities in our lives? I believe these five simple keys will help you in your quest for patience.

■ **1. Determine that you will never quit.** Before you begin any venture, determine in your heart and mind that YOU WILL NOT QUIT! When I became pastor of Mount Hope Church, I determined that I'd stay for 30 years. I believed I had the call of the Lord, and come what may — good, bad, or mediocre — I determined to stay.

The marriage covenant should be just like that, too. No one should go into a marriage thinking there is an escape hatch. Gary Uptigrove, our Care Pastor, talks about the "Marriage Satisfaction Curve." During the first months of marriage, the newlywed's sense of satisfaction with their marriage is high! Then, as the years pass, it starts gradually drifting down, like a feather to the ground. By the time many couples reach mid-life and their children are in their teenage years, they have become seriously dissatisfied with their marriages. Often this is the stage where many couples divorce.

After the divorce, they sometimes start over with a new spouse. For awhile everything is great, but the cycle begins again. By the time they reach their older years, many people discover they have spent their whole lives in marriages that never were very happy.

On the marriage satisfaction curve, it shows that after the children grow out of their teens, the satisfaction level in the marriage goes almost all the way back up to "honeymoon level."

What's the secret? Patience. Because when you develop patience and invest in your relationship, time will bring changes. Soon you will find yourself on the other side of the valley of discontentment and on a new pinnacle of loving satisfaction with your mate. God will reward your patience.

■ **2. Decide that God is completely and absolutely trustworthy, and He will always work things out for your good.** Imagine this. You are facing the Red Sea. The enemy presses hard on your heels. Soon they will fall upon you with their flashing swords and razor sharp lances. To either side loom high, rocky crags, impossible to scale. As you consider the foaming waves before you, the cries of your people are in your ears sounding like the thousands of gulls that swoop overhead. What, in God's name, are you going to do? Where, in this picture of crashing waves, lowering sky, cruel rocks, and merciless enemy, lays your escape?

What would have happened to the children of Israel, those many years ago, if Moses had doubted God's trustworthiness. What if Moses had said, "This is it, Lord. Everything you told me was a lie. Even You can't get me out of this." Things would have turned out very differently, I think. Doubt does not give God any room to work in our lives against our problems. But Moses didn't doubt. He trusted the Lord. As a result, the children of Israel were delivered in a most spectacular scene. The sea opened, and a path was made before them, and they walked to safety. God was continually working for their good. He knew exactly how to get the job done, and there was no way He could fail. In the same way, His love and care for us are perfect.

■ **3. Trust God for the courage to stand, even in the face of insurmountable odds.** That's what David did when he faced the mighty giant, Goliath. There was this huge, ugly giant taunting and teasing and cursing the children of Israel. Before him stood this little, ruddy-faced kid who said, "Who is this giant making all this noise and blaspheming God and His people? I'm going to take this giant down!"

"Sure," taunted his brothers, "you and what army?" But David wouldn't be dissuaded. He knew the Lord was on his side. He picked up five smooth rocks, loaded his slingshot, and let one fly. David aimed right for the weak spot in the giant's armor; his eye slot. With a screaming whistle, that rock flew through the air and hit that giant square between the eyes! Before Goliath knew what hit him, his head was neatly lopped from his shoulders!

David was the hero. People couldn't believe their eyes. But David knew that if God gave him the courage to stand against Goliath, He would make him a winner — even in the face of incredible odds.

What was true for David is just as true today. Mount Hope Church's ministries have touched so many lives. So many people have found Jesus, been delivered of addictions, turned away from degenerate life-styles, and found a new life in Jesus Christ. We have established several daughter churches and built many other churches in foreign countries. We are healing our community with the Word of God.

The story of Elijah, surrounded by enemies, illustrates how trusting in God for courage can work. There was Elijah, sitting in his easy chair reading the Bible. His servant ran in, distressed, nervous. "Oh master, master! We are surrounded by enemies. They've come to get us, to rip out our tongues and pop out our eyes! What can we do?" Elijah just calmly sat there. "Oh, Master, open this faithless servant's eyes to see what is really out there," Elijah prayed.

Suddenly, the scales were lifted from the servant's eyes, and he looked out. What he saw brought a smile of relief to his face. "Oh Master! There are flaming angels guarding all around the city, and those that are with us are more than those that are with them!"

Now, what that servant couldn't see with his natural eye was nevertheless very real. Greater is the number with us than the number against us! There are angels around everyone who fears the Lord. Stand up in the face of odds. Ask God for courage to stand against whatever comes against you, and then stand back and watch the miracles overtake you!

■ 4. **Remember the heat is only on to shape you and get you ready for a more powerful anointing, a bigger and greater use for God, or for a mighty miracle.** When the heat is really on and things get tough, patience is the key.

> "My brethren, count it all joy when ye fall into divers temptations; Knowing this, that the trying of your faith worketh patience. But let patience have her perfect work, that ye may be perfect and entire, wanting nothing."
>
> *James 1:2-4*

When the blacksmith has the piece of iron in the forge, the iron might find it a little hot. But when the blacksmith has finished working with the iron, it will be stronger, more beautiful, and more useful than it was before the heat was applied. In the same way, God tests us in the heat of troubles.

Many times I've felt like running from my own ministry, when the struggles, and resistance, and hurtful wagging tongues made me feel like getting out. I would stand on my promise to God. I would say, "Lord, I've committed this 30 years to you. I'm staying." Without fail, almost immediately, a new anointing or a bigger miracle would come into my life. Something big happened to me when I determined to allow God to shape me as long as the heat was on.

Blind Bartimaeus shouted, "Son of David, have mercy on me."

"Oh, leave the Master alone. He doesn't have time for you," scolded His disciples.

Bartimaeus could have given up, dropped out of church, and never come back. He could have taken offense and gone off in a huff. But he shouted all the louder, "Jesus! Son of David, have mercy on me!"

"What do you want?" queried Jesus.

"I want my sight!"

"By your faith, be it unto you," Jesus said.

"I can see!" exulted Bartimaeus.

That was persistence. That was tenacity. That was refusing to let go until the promise was fulfilled.

■ **5. Make a faith pact between God and yourself.** Write it down in your prayer journal or on a card taped to your mirror where you can see it every day. Here is what you should write on that card, and don't forget to sign it.

"I will never surrender to discouragement. I will never surrender to despair because Jesus is with me and has promised to never leave me nor forsake me."

Jesus came to this earth to be one of us. He showed us what our Father is like. Jesus died on the cross, a common criminal's execution. Yet, He was sinless. It looked like the greatest defeat for His ministry. And it would have been if God had stopped there.

But He didn't. He was patient. He persevered. And on the third day — even death could not defeat Him! Jesus proved it. He came out of the tomb on the third day for our justification. So when it looks like all is lost, when you are going down in flames, remember — God will always turn it around to be your greatest victory or biggest miracle.

I know, by the Holy Ghost, that you need patience. You may feel like you are being overwhelmed, swallowed up in your problems, defeated by despair. What you need is patience. Stand on your faith, and patiently wait for God to work His will in your life. He will solve your problems. He promised.

Chapter Thirty

ADDITIVE #7: GODLINESS – EUSEBEIA

"HEAVENLY MINDED, DOWN TO EARTH" WORD

By Dick Mills

Godliness can be also godlikeness. Having reverence toward the Lord and aspiring to be like Him is "godlikeness." Words like: "Be Holy for I am Holy," and "Forgiving one another even as the Lord has forgiven you," and "Be merciful as your Father also is merciful," demonstrate our capability to acquire godlike qualities. The very word "Christian" means a miniature Christ or a reflection of Jesus.

With EUSEBEIA we love the way Jesus loves, we talk the way He talks, we walk the way He walks, we care for people the way He cares for people, and we reach out and touch people the way He touched them. EUSEBEIA states with Paul (2 Corinthians 4:11) that, "The life of Jesus also may be manifested in our mortal flesh." EUSEBEIA looks to the Lord Jesus Christ as our ideal or role-model and our example.

EUSEBEIA (yoo-seb-i-ah), Strong's #2150, appears 15 times in the Greek New Testament. The word is a compound of "eu"—well or good, and "sebomai"— to be devout.

EUSEBEIA is a right disposition towards God. It is reverence directed towards the Lord. It is an attitude which is well pleasing to Him. It is the opposite of an ungodly walk. J.N. Darby defines the word as "a heart that is in communion with the Lord." J. Neiboer states of EUSEBEIA, "Godliness is really an inward virtue, but it manifests itself outwardly by a life of service. It gives a believer a strong desire to be Christ-like."

God-fearing needs to be defined. There is a fear that is cowering, quivering, shrinking, and cowardly. This is also called "guilty fear." It was evidenced by Adam and Eve hiding from the Lord with frightened trepidation. Another fear is based on reverential awe. It is a fear of displeasing the one who loves us so much. God-fearing is that kind of fear. It is a wholesome respect that is determined to keep His commandments and do those things that are pleasing in His sight.

"GODLINESS"

TRANSLATIONS

Living Bible — *Patient and godly*

Godbey — *Holiness to live*

Ledyard — *Godlike*

Fenton — *Obedience*

J.B. Phillips — *Devotion to God*

Basic English — *The fear of God*

Laubach — *Serve God*

Concordant — *Devoutness*

A. Cressman — *Be true to God*

Jerusalem Bible — *True devotion*

Ballantine — *Reverence*

Amplified — *Piety*

The Deaf N.T. — *Service for God*

"EUSEBEIA is the pathway to the real profit and the real joy in this world and in the world to come (1 Timothy 4:8). True happiness never results from the possession of things. It is not in things to give either satisfaction or peace. True happiness lies entirely in personal relationships. If a man has love, he has everything. The greatest of all personal relationships is the relationship with God. When that relationship is right, then life is true happiness."
—William Barclay

Chapter Thirty-One

GODLINESS

By Dave Williams

"And to knowledge temperance; and to temperance patience; and to patience godliness..."

2 Peter 1:6

In our quest to become high performance believers, we have looked at six of the nine additives that will immeasurably empower our walk with Jesus. When these qualities are present, life is exciting and successful. When they are absent, life is boring, burdensome, and lacking in joy. Each one of these qualities are important and indispensible in constructing a victorious life.

Let's review the additives.

■ **1. Diligence — the get-going ingredient.**

■ 2. Faith — the ingredient that turns impossibilities into possibilities, mistakes into miracles.

■ 3. Virtue — the commitment to quality ingredient.

■ 4. Knowledge — the getting-to-know God ingredient.

■ 5. Temperance — the ingredient that brings self-control.

■ 6. Patience — the hang-in there ingredient.

The next vital element in the recipe for success is godliness.

What is godliness? You hear a lot of terms in church that are sometimes poorly understood. Words like righteousness, holiness, and godliness tend to get lumped together as if they all mean the same thing, but really they don't.

Righteousness has two definitions: first, it means a right standing with God that only comes by faith in Jesus Christ. Second, it means a right standing with man that only comes by working at it. Holiness is purity of thought, word, and deed.

Godliness means being like God.

I read a story about a young boy. He was toiling down the road carrying a bulky bag of apples. Suddenly, he stumbled and pitched forward into the thoroughfare, scattering apples in all directions. Struggling to his feet, he began frantically gathering his apples. All around him pandemonium reigned. Horns blared; people shouted — but not one person offered to help the poor boy collect his apples. Then an old man saw the child's plight and began to help him get the fruit back into the bag. When they were finished, the little guy looked up and asked, "Hey, mister, are you God?" That's godliness — when people see God through you because of your actions.

Godliness is godlikeness. It's not an automatic gift that comes when you are first saved anymore than a good physique is given to you automatically when you come to Christ. Godliness is something that you learn. It is expressed by acts of kindness, mercy, goodness, courtesy, and caring — even to those who don't deserve it or are strangers to us. Godliness is courteous and kindly service to others.

That is why I continually encourage and motivate Christians to become involved in some kind of ministry. Unless you are serving others, it is very difficult, if not impossible, to develop the quality of godliness.

In the Bible, we are told to seek the face of God. I believe that this means drawing so close to God that our very face is transformed with His radiance. The Greek translation of the word godliness shows a picture of a superior bending down in loving kindness to help an inferior. It's reaching down to lift someone up with a kind word or a loving deed — regardless of whether or not that person has done anything to deserve the consideration.

That is what Jesus did for us. While we were yet sinners, totally unworthy of his concern, He stepped across the universe of eternity and became one of us. Why? So that He could live, suffer, and die. That He might be resurrected and ascend into heaven and stand before our Heavenly Father's throne, imputing to each of us His own justification. Jesus demonstrated godliness. He showed us what God is like.

Godliness is the opposite of evil, corruption, profanity, and wickedness. Whenever you read in the Bible about the wicked, just turn it around to the opposite, and you will find godliness. If it says the ungodly are always digging up evil, then you know the reverse is true of the godly. They are covering the faults of others. When the Bible says the ungodly are like chaff blowing away in the wind (Psalm 1), then you'll know the reverse is true of the godly. They are stable and secure. When it says the ungodly will not be able to stand during the judgment, then when the judgment comes, the godly will be left standing.

How will godliness benefit your life?

Chapter Thirty-Two

BENEFITS OF GODLINESS

By Dave Williams

■ **1. Godliness promises to deliver you.** God has promised the believer who grows in godliness a supernatural deliverance. "The Lord knows how to deliver the godly out of temptation," (2 Peter 2:9). The word temptation not only means enticement to do evil, but it also means trouble and trials. Have you ever faced trouble in your life? Deep trouble? How often was it your own fault? If you develop the additive of godliness, God will always give you a way of escape. He knows exactly how to get you out of any mess you've made for yourself. So, to develop godliness, you do the same for others. You be willing to stoop down and extend a helping hand — deserved or not.

■ **2. You will profit now.** "Godliness will profit you," (1 Timothy 4:8). I know of three Christian women who took jobs in a secretarial pool at a mega-corporation. The first day they reported for work, they were taken to a large room filled with desks. At each desk, a woman was busily working. No one greeted them, smiled, or even looked up. Later, one of the newcomers had a question and approached one of the older secretaries. The response was not what she expected. "Look," the older secretary snapped, "that's not my job. I can't do my job and your's too. You were hired to do it, so do it!"

At lunch, the three Christians discussed the situation. One said, "What can we do? This is a terrible place to work. Let's just go with the flow and don't do anything we're not paid to do."

"No," stated another. "Godliness means doing nice things for people even when they don't deserve it." So after lunch, they went back to the office with a strategy. They brought everyone a soda. They smiled and said pleasant things to all the other workers. One saw work piling up on another's desk and offered to work through the afternoon break to help her catch up. The other employees didn't know what to think!

For two weeks they kept this up. Then, something happened. Suddenly, the original employees came forward with offers to help when one of the Christian women fell behind. People began to smile, and a spirit of cooperation and harmony filled the office. Godliness had done its wonderful work!

You can make godliness work in your life too. It can turn your life around. You will profit from godliness.

A former associate pastor at Mount Hope Church, Robin Clair, tells this story about Herman Rhode. Herman was the District Superintendent for our denomination in Minnesota when Robin and his wife, Judy, were just beginning in the ministry there. One day there was a knock at the door of their little back-woods parsonage. When Robin opened the door, there stood Herman, tall and distinguished — a successful shepherd of over 600 churches! Herman pulled out his checkbook and said, "Come on! Let's go grocery shopping; I want to be sure you have enough food."

Years later, Robin saw Herman Rhode and said to him, "Brother Rhode, I don't remember any of the sermons you preached, but I will never forget that one act of kindness that you did for me when you really didn't have to."

The superior had stooped down to help one of his subordinates in need. Herman Rhode went on to be elected as one of the thirteen national Executive Presbyters of the Assemblies of God. Not only that, in recognition for his many kind and generous deeds, he was awarded an honorary doctorate degree from North Central Bible College. Godliness certainly profited him. It will profit you also.

■ **3. Godliness will also bring great gain.**

"If any man teach otherwise,
and consent not to wholesome

> *words, even the words of our Lord
> Jesus Christ, and to the doctrine
> which is according to godliness; he
> is proud, knowing nothing, but dot-
> ing about questions and strifes of
> words, whereof cometh envy, strife,
> railings, evil surmisings; perverse
> disputings of men of corrupt minds,
> and destitute of the truth, suppos-
> ing that gain is godliness: from such
> withdraw thyself. But godliness
> with contentment is great gain."*
>
> 1 Timothy 6:3-6

Could you use some gain in your life? These verses, believe it or not, are referring to material gain. If you go after material gain alone, you are going to be disappointed. But if you seek godliness with contentment, you will receive great gain! Go after money alone and you'll get ungodliness. Go after godliness and you'll get godliness and opportunities for material gain as well.

Consider Jesus. Can you imagine what it must have been like for Him knowing that in a few days He would be going to His execution? He would be publicly humiliated, tied to a whipping post, and flogged with metal and bone-tipped leather strips until the blood ran. His beard would be ripped out by the roots! He could have been obsessed by fears for Himself. Instead, He demonstrated godliness by His concern for others. He washed the feet of His disciples! He offered them comfort, even in His darkest hour.

Then consider the Sunday following His death. If you don't think godliness brings great gain, consider His resurrection.

When you're in trouble and having problems, who do you think about? Yourself! Everyone wants to have an Easter Sunday, but nobody wants to have a part in the painful ordeal of Good Friday. But when you reach out to others, even in the midst of your trouble, you demonstrate godliness, and there will be an Easter Sunday for you.

How do you develop godliness in your life?

Chapter Thirty-Three
DEVELOPING GODLINESS
By Dave Williams

Everyone is being very vocal about their rights these days. But the Bible says, he who seeks to save his own life will lose it. Jesus was the Son of God. He could have called a legion of angels to rescue Him, but He didn't. He gave up His rights. Until we give up our drive to always put ourselves and our needs first, we will never be able to develop godliness in our characters.

■ **1. Resolve to give up your "rights."** One time a four-teen-year-old boy came up to me and put his hand on my shoulder and said, "How's it going, Dave."

Horrified, his father pulled him away and scolded him for taking the liberty of calling me "Dave" instead of "Pastor Williams." Well, Dave is my name! When people call me Pastor Williams, I think they're upset with me. I'm sure that the children who came up to Jesus didn't call Him "Mr. Messiah," or "Reverend Christ." They probably called Him "Jesus." They knew He loved them and loved ministering to them. Jesus was a humble man never placing Himself above others. He was Lord of all creation, yet He emptied Himself to become one of us.

I read a story about some soldiers who were trying to load heavy logs on a truck during WWII. They were having a terrible time getting the job done; the logs were so heavy. A man walked up and surveyed the scene. He approached the Sergeant in charge and asked, "Hey, what's going on here?"

"They're trying to load those logs," gruffed the Sergeant.

"Well, why aren't you helping them?"

"Because I'm the Sergeant, and they're the privates; that's why."

So the inquiring man walked over and started helping the privates load the logs. When the job was done, the Sergeant inquired, "Hey, who are you anyway?"

"I'm General Eisenhower."

Everyone would agree that General Eisenhower received great promotion and great gain. He became President of the United States. If you want to develop godliness, give up your rights.

■ **2. Read the right books.** If I could see your library, I could instantly tell where you fall on the godliness scale. Are you wasting your time reading trashy romance novels or bloody murder mysteries? Or are you seeking to learn more about your Heavenly Father. Read something that will benefit you.

■ **3. Listen to the right people.** Some people are always ripping others apart — wasting time in gossip and idle speculation. These people have bitter spirits, are cranky, and have bad attitudes. They will only drag you down to their level. Godliness is being able to speak gentle words about somebody even when you disagree with them. Listen to the right people.

■ **4. Say the right words.** I don't always feel like saying the right words, especially when I feel upset or unhappy with someone! But if I want to develop godliness, I must say the right words — kind words, honest words, God's words.

■ **5. Do the right thing.** A Jew was heading for Jerusalem on the dangerous Jericho road. He should have known better, but this was a shortcut, and he was in a hurry. He walked right into trouble, was attacked, robbed, beaten, and left almost dead on the side of the road. Finally a pastor came along. "Praise God," the injured man thought, "here is help!"

But the pastor looked at the bloody, battered man and thought, "Oh no! If I touch him, I will become ceremonially unclean and won't be able to go to church. Please God, send someone else to help this man." So the pastor passed him by.

Then came a deacon, hurrying along, late for church. He saw the man but quickly crossed over to the other side of the road pretending not to see him.

Then, along came a Samaritan. Samaritans were despised by the Jews. There were political and racial tensions between them. The man's hopes were shattered. "If my own people won't lift a hand to help me, surely this Samaritan won't stop to help."

But the Samaritan did stop. He lifted the man's head and anointed it with oil. He cleansed his wounds and bound them up. He placed the man on his own donkey and took him to an inn and paid for his room for two months. The Samaritan told the innkeeper, "Take care of this man until he is well, and if I owe you more money, I'll pay you on my next trip through." What an example of godliness!

You see, godliness is an exercise. Paul told Timothy to exercise himself unto godliness. In other words, it won't just happen, you have to work at it.

There once was a young man who worked for a Christian in a lumberyard. The owner was a believer, but he was not an easy boss. One day, the young man got angry with his boss and quit.

He started his own lumber company. He didn't run his business in an ethical manner. He raided his old boss' client list and unfairly undercut his prices. He was trying to drive his old boss out of business by any means possible. It was hard on the Christian businessman as his business dwindled.

Then one morning, the young man came to his lumberyard and found it in flames. He lost every bit of his stock. He couldn't fill his orders or meet his deadlines. He sat in his office in despair sure he would lose everything.

He looked out the window and saw his old boss' truck pull in. He thought, "Here he comes to gloat at my failure."

But the old man came in and put his arm around the young man's shoulders. "I'm so sorry this happened. Take all the lumber you need from my yard to fill your orders, and you can pay me when you're able. Get yourself back on your feet again."

There is an example of godliness! Even though that young man didn't deserve help, the Christian freely gave it. He did the right thing.

■ **6. Associate with the right people.** There is a lot to be said about your associations. If you associate with godly people, it will rub off. If you associate with bad people, that too will rub off. It is like the man who entered his donkey in the Kentucky Derby. "You entered your donkey in the Kentucky Derby," said someone in amazement. "You know it doesn't have a chance of winning."

"Yeah, I know, but I thought the associations would do him a lot of good."

We do become like the people we run around with. If you want to develop godliness, start rubbing shoulders with godly people.

■ **7. Ask God to give you whatever you need to become more like Him.** God will never force you to be more like Him, but He will always help you if you ask.

Remember, developing godliness is an exercise. You must practice it. Start by doing something this week for someone who doesn't deserve it. Offer to help the widow next door; reach out and do something to make some situation better. And then, speak gently to someone. The next time you disagree with someone, don't lose your temper and insist on your own way. Speak quietly and softly, and sense the feeling of peace that will enter your heart when you keep your temper.

You will be amazed at what godliness will bring to your life. It will help speed you down the road toward your destination of becoming a high performance believer!

Chapter Thirty-Four
ADDITIVE #8: BROTHERLY KINDNESS —
PHILADELPHIA
"CARING FOR THE BROTHERHOOD"
By Dick Mills

Each country in the world has its own geographical boundaries, its own language, its own family culture, its own life-style. Sweden is a country. Sweden has a language. Sweden has its families and its way of life. Italy is a country. Italian is its language. The Italian family is its distinctive feature, and the Italian way of life is very recognizable. Christianity likewise has its unique country; it is called the Kingdom of God. We speak our own language. It is the language of faith, hope, and love (1 Corinthians 13:13). Some Christians at conversion lose 75 percent of their former vocabulary as they acquire the new language. We also have our culture and our way of life (remember the chorus, "I found a new way of living?").

One of the joys of salvation is our new Christian families, our brothers and sisters, our fathers and mothers, our friends. Now that you are in the company of the redeemed, you have millions of new friends you have not even met yet. It is the family of Christ. PHILADELPHIA is the key word to all this.

PHILADELPHIA (fill-add-ell-fee-ah), Strong's #5360, is a compound of two words: "phileo"— to love, and "adelphos" — from the same source, or having the same parentage. "Adelphos" also means from the same womb or from the same origin.

Checking the Greek lexicons does not give us too many alternatives or too much variety since the word is so self-explanatory. Souter defines it, "Love of fellow Christians since we are all sons of the same Father in a special sense."

Thayer states, "Agape love in the New Testament is the love which Christians cherish for each other as brethren." Bullinger tersely defines it, "Brotherly love." The United Bible Society in its translators guide did say this of PHILA-DELPHIA, "In non-biblical contexts, this term would refer to affection or love for persons belonging to a so-called in-group (Fraternity, Lodge, Club, etc.). However, in the New Testament, this in-group is defined in terms of Christian faith." Kittel calls it, "The Spiritual Brotherhood."

"BROTHERLY KINDNESS"

TRANSLATIONS

New RSV — *Mutual affection*

Knox — *Brotherly love*

Norlie — *Brotherliness*

Barclay — *Christian friendliness*

Douay — *Fraternal love*

Jerusalem Bible — *Kindness toward your fellow men*

Concordant — *Brotherly fondness*

Goodspeed — *With a spirit of brotherhood*

Living Bible — *For you to enjoy other people and to like them*

New American — *Care for your brother*

Wuest — *An affection for the brethren*

Ledyard — *Be kind to Christian brothers and love them*

"PHILADELPHIA is a tender affection to all our fellow Christians. We are children of the same Father. We are servants of the same Master, members of the same family and travellers to the same country. We are helpers of the same inheritance and, therefore, are to be loved with a pure and fervent heart."

—Matthew Henry

Chapter Thirty-Five
BROTHERLY KINDNESS
By Dave Williams

"And to godliness brotherly kindness; and to brotherly kindness charity."

2 Peter 1:7

It's true that we live in a cruel world. Every day the newspapers and TV are filled with stories about man's cruelty to others. In Rwanda, hundreds of thousands have been slaughtered simply because they're members of the wrong tribe. An article in the paper told of a babysitter who put a tiny baby into a microwave and turned it on! Examples of the cruelty of which man is capable are endless. Most people find this kind of behavior incomprehensible.

My daughter is so kind that we can't drive into the driveway when it rains without moving the worms off the driveway first. Worm rescue! Our property must have more worms than anywhere else in the neighborhood. They know where they'll be protected. Then there are other people who will go out of their way to run over frogs in the road after it rains. If a policeman ever followed me after a rain, I don't know what he would think, as I weave about trying to miss the frogs.

In our homes, our churches, our work places, our country, and our world, it is too easy to find examples of cruelty and indifference. If we want to develop a high powered life, we must reverse that by developing and refining the habit of kindness.

We are on a journey of discovery learning how to build a high performance life. It's not an easy, overnight process that can be achieved in a few days. We cannot have perfect knowledge of God in an instant, and walking in faith requires the development of faith muscles and exercises in patience.

Like a good builder, we must dig the foundation of our faith deeply, searching God's Word and meditating on its truth until it becomes strong within us. Each day brings us new opportunities to draw closer to Him until our faith becomes so strong, so unshakable, that not even the biggest storm of life can disturb our faith in Him and our love for Him.

At times, it may seem that you are stuck in the slow lane watching others race by in their spiritual growth.

Don't be discouraged! Like the wise man who built his house on the rock, your house will be safe. Even though it took much longer to dig down into that rock; when the house was done, it was invincible! The person who seems to be achieving spiritual excellence overnight may have neglected digging his spiritual foundations. He might have built for speed, not for excellence, and the first high wind may find his house in shambles.

Think of the Taj Mahal. The largest mausoleum in the world took more than thirteen years to complete. Twenty thousand men labored those many years to finish that building, and it has stood since 1645!

Adding kindness to the other qualities we have already discussed will take your spiritual foundation even deeper, assuring you victory in your quest for high performance living.

"Put on therefore, as the elect of God, holy and beloved, bowels of mercies, kindness, humbleness of mind, meekness, longsuffering; Forbearing one another, and forgiving one another, if any man have a quarrel against any: even as Christ forgave you, so also do ye."

Colossians 3:12-13

In the Hebrew, brotherly kindness has a beautiful definition. It means beauty, mercy, and good deeds. The Hebrews actually believed that if you were kind to others, you would become a more beautiful person. In fact, that's the way it's paraphrased in The Living Bible in the book of Proverbs. "Kindness makes a person beautiful." Have you ever noticed how that is really true?

When I was sixteen years old, I was in a singing group, and we cut a record on the giant label "Key Records" out of Kalamazoo, Michigan. We had 500 copies made of that record; we were going national — we were hitting the big time! The radio station in Jackson, Michigan, played our record, and some of the local stores carried it. We were taking orders from all our relatives. I needed envelopes to mail the records to my out-of-town relatives, so I went to an office supply store to get mailing envelopes.

The store clerk was unimpressed. He said I would never be able to find what I wanted — nobody made anything like that — and turned away to help another customer. It was obvious he thought I was just some kid who didn't deserve his consideration and that helping me was just a waste of his time. Adults often treat children like that, but kids are important and should always be treated kindly.

So I tried another store. The owner came and introduced himself to me and treated me like I was his most important customer. I told him I'd just cut a record. He acted very impressed. He even wanted to buy a copy! When I told him I wanted envelopes to mail some records to relatives, his response was, "Let's see what we can do. I don't have the exact size you're looking for, but I've got these slightly larger ones, and I think you could fold and tape them to fit." I took 100 envelopes, and that encounter was the beginning of a real friendship.

I would go almost every day to the store and buy some little thing, like a pencil or a roll of tickets. If I ever heard of anyone needing office supplies, I always recommended that store. The owner and his wife always took a kind interest in me. Even after I'd gone into the U.S. Navy, I would visit the store whenever I was in town. Their unfailing kindness made the owner and his wife beautiful people.

The opposite of brotherly kindness is aloofness. That means that you don't care about me, and I don't care about you. You don't have time for, or interest in, anyone else. Aloofness is a form of rudeness. It is especially bad in business situations. When you are in business, the customer should be your primary concern, and you should go out of your way to be kind and helpful to him. Recently, I took my wife to a very "elegant" restaurant in Grand Rapids. It was a hamburger joint. As usual, I wanted Coney Dogs; she wanted a cheeseburger. The cashier totalled our order before we had a chance to request a beverage. She acted like this was a big problem for her, and when I asked for iced tea, she implied that I should have known the iced tea machine was off. Her attitude made it easy for me to take this particular place off my list of "favorite food stops."

Hostility is also the opposite of kindness. There are work places, homes, even churches, where you sense a hostile atmosphere the moment you enter the door. Nobody is smiling; nobody is having any fun. There are factions and cliques, and a mean spirited attitude prevails.

Back in the 1960's, when American schools were being desegregated, there was a spirit of fear and hostility in many schools. Parents were afraid. Black parents were afraid to send their children to school with white children for fear that their children would be hurt; and white parents were afraid to send their children to school with black children for the same reason. The parents' fears and attitudes were transmitted to the children, so the children were afraid too. One mother picked up her little daughter after school one day and said, "Honey, did you have to sit next to any colored children today?" "Yes, Mommy," she said. "I sat beside this little black girl. We were both so afraid that there was going to be a riot we held hands during the whole class!"

Brotherly kindness is the opposite of hostility. One church denomination is hostile to another. This is ridiculous! We all worship one God and one Savior, Jesus Christ. We are all in fraternal fellowship because we are all members of the same Body.

Stinginess, pettiness, harshness, and thoughtlessness are all antonyms of brotherly kindness. In these days of cruel violence and crass indifference to suffering, we must all reach out to one another with love. If we don't, we will soon be living like jungle animals. It was Jesus who showed us a perfect example of how to express brotherly kindness for *all* people, and we can emulate Him. How would Jesus behave toward others if He were walking the earth today? The next chapter describes some good ways to start.

Chapter Thirty-Six
APPLYING BROTHERLY KINDNESS
By Dave Williams

Where can you exercise brotherly kindness?

■ **1. In church.** We all belong to one another. Paul said to beware, lest we bite and devour, and thus destroy one another. At church we're a family, and there must be brotherly kindness.

■ **2. At home.** Members of the same family are in fraternal fellowship with one another. If the home is to be happy and harmonious, then every member must be treated with kindness and consideration. So many homes aren't happy because there is a lack of brotherly kindness between its members.

■ **3. In the work place.** At work everyone is employed by the same boss; everyone is involved in attaining a common goal. Once again, all employees make up a fraternal fellowship and should be treated with kindness and consideration.

We have been hearing a lot about the problems among workers in the postal service. In recent years more than 14 people have been murdered by disgruntled postal workers. If you read the news articles concerning these murders, the common thread that runs through these tragic stories is poor management.

It seems there wasn't much kindness on the part of management to these employees. They managed by threat and intimidation rather than kindness. There was no spirit of fraternal kindness and cooperation, no feeling of compassion or caring. The Bible says that perfect love casts out fear, so fear must bring hatred. When someone fears you, they hate you. And in hatred grows the seed of murder.

This is no excuse for those who shot down innocent people in cold blood. But if there had been an atmosphere of brotherly kindness rather than fear and hatred, maybe these tragic murders would never have taken place!

I have a "Pastor's Minute" radio show on a local radio station, WITL. I have never seen any secular work place where there is so much brotherly kindness and camaraderie. They are a team — working together, laughing together, loyal to each other. There is a spirit of loving kindness there. I have never heard a single negative comment from any employee regarding the station owner or manager. He has masterfully created a climate of brotherly kindness among his workers. It is the kind of atmosphere that should exist in every home, church, and work place. Wouldn't it be great if your home, job, and church were places where the people there were your biggest, most loyal supporters? Wouldn't it be wonderful if everyone you knew would be the last person to think the worst about you?

Face it, underneath the superficial differences of skin color, or sex, or age, we are all cousins — we all go back to Noah and his wife. We have a fraternal fellowship in the human race! Peter says one of the keys for high performance living is fraternal kindness for one another.

Another aspect of brotherly kindness is to keep yourself from sending out signals of seduction; don't create an atmosphere of flirtation. I have talked to ministers all over the country, and so many of them tell me they constantly fight against temptations. They tell me that women are constantly trying to seduce them. It's hard for me to understand because this just doesn't happen to me! In fact, I prayed about it, "Lord, either I am too stupid to sense these lures, or I'm just too ugly to attract them." But the Lord spoke to my heart and said, "Dave, you're not stupid or ugly; you're just not sending out flirtatious signals, and those other men are." Don't send out seductive signals; it's not brotherly kindness to do that.

There are other common courtesies that are often overlooked. For instance, don't whisper. When I am preaching and see someone whisper, it makes me wonder if something is wrong. I'm sure others feel the same way. Also, when you are talking to someone, give them your full attention. Don't interrupt, and don't finish their sentences for them. Be courteous and kind.

Also, treat members of the opposite sex with proper etiquette. I know men can sometimes be crude, especially with each other. I was in a restaurant once, and seated next to me was a well dressed man and woman having a conversation. If I had been the woman, I would have gotten up and walked out! He had no respect for her. He used every three, four, and seven letter word in the book.

If you must repeat something about someone, make sure you put it in the best possible light, especially if you don't have all the facts. Gossip is not kind.

Don't be habitually late. If you are consistently late, it shows that you have no respect for other people and their time. It is not a kind way of treating others.

What will striving to add brotherly kindness to our lives do for us, and why is it important? The next chapter will show what this vital "additive" will bring to your life.

Chapter Thirty-Seven
WHAT KINDNESS BRINGS
By Dave Williams

What does the development of the trait of brotherly kindness bring to our lives? Why do we need it to be high performance believers?

■ **1. We belong to one another.**

> *"Let us hold fast the profession of our faith without wavering; (for He is faithful that promised;) and let us consider one another to provoke unto love and to good works: not forsaking the assembling of ourselves together, as the manner of some is; but exhorting one another: and so much the more, as ye see the day approaching."*

> *Hebrews 10:23-25*

How do we express the belief that we belong to one another in Christ's Body, that we're all a part of each other? First of all, by being there. I go to a lot of meetings that I don't really need to go to. I don't really need to go to another sectional or district council meeting. But I found something out. They need me. Part of Christian maturity is doing things not because you need to but because someone else needs you to.

A woman was declared legally blind by her doctor. Her boyfriend literally dragged her to church. She came to the altar for healing, and one of the healing team members was impressed by the Holy Spirit and laid hands on her. Her blindness was healed! What if that healing team member hadn't bothered to come and minister that day? She came to be used of God, not out of selfish motivations.

If you feel a lack in your life, that you are not being spiritually fed where you are, examine yourself. Are you reaching out and ministering to others? Are you tithing? If you're not reaching out in ministry to others, you're probably not being fed because your life is a swamp instead of a mighty river with direction. If you want God to flow into you and through your life, you have to let Him flow from you to others.

■ **2. We express brotherly kindness by participating.** Maybe God will call you to reach out to someone like He called that healing team member to reach out to the blind woman. Obey His direction for your life. Find your special gift and use it in His service. Become an active, moving member of the Body of Christ! Maybe you should start a Bible study in your home. Maybe He is calling you to reflect Christ's attitudes in your life at work, thereby changing your work place from hostility to happiness. God has gifted each and every one of us in some marvelous way. Find your gift and use it.

> *"For, brethren, ye have been called unto liberty; only use not liberty for an occasion to the flesh, but by love serve one another. For all the law is fulfilled in one word, even in this; Thou shalt love thy neighbor as thyself."*
>
> Galatians 5:13-14

There are great benefits to brotherly kindness.

First, a multiplied return. What you sow, you reap. When you sow kindness in other people's lives, you will reap kindness in return. Do you remember the story of Rebekah? Abraham's servant went to look for a wife for Isaac. He was a wealthy man, a really good catch, and the servant was anxious to find a good wife for him. He determined that if a woman showed him a kindness, he would know that she was the right one. So what did Rebekah do? As the servant sat by the well, Rebekah offered to bring him and all his animals water. What did this kind act bring to her? She was covered with jewels, became the wife of a wealthy man and the mother of Israel! Her kindness was certainly multiplied back to her many times.

The second benefit of brotherly love is honor.

> *"And he said, Blessed be thou of the Lord, my daughter: for thou hast shewed more kindness in the latter end than at the beginning, inasmuch as thou followedst not young men, whether poor or rich. And now, my daughter, fear not; I will do to thee all that thou requirest: for all the city of my people doth know that thou art a virtuous woman."*

> *Ruth 3:10-11*

Ruth was honored because of her kindness. Because of her actions she became the wife of wealthy Boaz and became part of the lineage of the Messiah.

The third benefit is wealth. Brotherly kindness can directly bring wealth. Nordstrom's on the West coast is a store that really believes in being kind to customers. Even though their prices are about 20 percent higher than stores with similar merchandise, they do more than four times the business of their competitors. Why? Because at Nordstrom's, the customer is king. Everyone is treated kindly. If you are dissatisfied with anything you purchased, they will take it back, no questions asked.

One time a woman came in and wanted to buy just a box. She said, "I am buying my friend a sweater for a gift, and I really want to give it to her in a Nordstrom's box, but the sweater I can afford is at the store next door." The cashier closed down her register, went next door and purchased the sweater, came back and sold it to the woman for the same price, and then wrapped it up in a Nordstrom's box. That is the practice of brotherly kindness. And it shows in Nordstrom's healthy profits!

Brotherly kindness can bring us multiplied returns, honor, and even wealth. Has God made you warmhearted, friendly, generous, helpful, and considerate? Like it or not, we belong to one another. We must develop these traits if we want to live happy, high powered Christian lives.

How do we do it? By reaching out to one another on a one-on-one basis. By joining small groups and participating. By working to become a part of it all. It is so easy to sit back in isolation with a critical attitude; but the person who reaches out, investing a part of himself in caring for others, is the person whose life will be enriched by the returning flood of the brotherly love of others.

Chapter Thirty-Eight
ADDITIVE #9: LOVE — AGAPE
"I ONLY WANT WHAT IS BEST FOR YOU"
WORD
By Dick Mills

The Greeks had four very interesting words for love: EROS, STORGE, PHILIA, and AGAPE. Each word was significant in our relationship with our fellow man (and woman) plus our relationship with God.

When Alexander the Great conquered the Mediterranean region (Circa 250-275 BC), "eros" was a colorful word describing married love. "Eros" conveyed passion, devotion, affection, and warmth. Unfortunately within a 250 year period, "eros" came to have a more unsavory meaning, and New Testament Bible writers did not use the term at all. Song of Solomon in the Greek Old Testament used the term, but New Testament writers avoided the word.

William Barclay states, "Eros as a word never got converted." Today "erotic" and "erotica" discolor the word.

"Storge" has to do with family love. It is a sort of "blood is thicker than water" mind set. "Storge" is used only once in the Greek New Testament, but only in a compound; "philostorgos"— "kindly affectionate." "Astorgos" appears twice in the New Testament as "without natural affection." So embodied within the word "storge" is an intense family love.

"Philia" is a love with feelings. It is also the Greek word for "kiss." It is easy to see that "philia" the noun and "phileo" the verb describe a word with a lot of warmth in it.

AGAPE has been defined by Hermann Cremer as a word, "Designating a love unknown to writers outside of the New Testament." Archbishop Trench states, "AGAPE is a word born within the bosom of revealed religion!" W.E. Vines says of AGAPE, "It is the characteristic word of Christianity." Arndt-Gingrich calls AGAPE, "The highest Christian virtue."

AGAPE (ag-ah-pay), Strong's #26, appears 115 times in the New Testament. One grammarian defined AGAPE as "a self-giving love that gives freely without asking anything in return." E.W. Bullinger describes AGAPE in these words, "AGAPE denotes the love which springs from admiration and veneration. AGAPE love chooses its object with a decision of the will. Then AGAPE love devotes a self-denying and compassionate devotion to that object. AGAPE is love in its fullest conceivable form." AGAPE is a love that flows unselfishly from a generous, caring heart.

Love can be known only from the actions it prompts. God's love is seen in the gift of His Son.

Christian love is not an impulse from the feelings. It does not always run with the natural inclinations. It does not spend itself only upon those for whom some affinity is discovered.

"CHARITY"

TRANSLATIONS

Amplified — *Christian love*

Basic English — *Love itself*

Douay — *Charity*

Living Bible — *Grow to love them deeply*

A. Cressman — *Love everyone*

Simple English — *Unselfish concern*

"Love seeks the welfare of all. It works no ill to anyone. Love seeks opportunity to do good to all men and especially toward them that are of the household of the faith."

— *Galatians 6:10*

Chapter Thirty-Nine

BROTHERLY LOVE

By Dave Williams

"And to godliness brotherly kindness; and to brotherly kindness charity."

2 Peter 1:7

We have come to the final additive for high performance living. God has promised us that when we work to develop these qualities, we will always have vision; we will never fail — we will always be victorious. When our faith is embellished with these nine additives, we know that our entrance into heaven will be triumphant; Jesus will be there to speak the words every Christian longs to hear, "Well done, good and faithful servant!"

The final additive is charity or brotherly love. You may not be able to sing like Amy Grant. You may not be able to preach like Billy Graham. You may not be able to see signs and wonders like Benny Hinn, pray like Dick Eastman, or prophesy like Dick Mills. But there is one thing you, and *every* believer can do — you can love people with the love of Jesus Christ.

This world exists in the kind of darkness that makes its victims less lovely every day. There are traps, snares, and pitfalls along life's road just waiting for the unwary. And when someone stumbles, it would be so easy for us to say, "It's not my problem; they should have known better." But that would not be Jesus' reaction. He came for sinners. He came for the suffering. He reached out to everyone no matter how ugly their sin. He would look at the unlovely sinner today with love in His eyes, and He wants us to do the same. Sinners are looking to us, the followers of Jesus Christ, to show them the meaning of real love.

The word charity actually means agape which is the deepest form of love that anyone can ever know. It doesn't mean taking up a collection for the orphanage or collecting canned goods for the food bank or clothes for the Salvation Army — although those are good things to do and should be done regularly. Yes, those could be called acts of charity, but in this sense, the word means more. It means God's perfect love working through us.

What is God's perfect love? A young man was writing to his girlfriend. He said, "Darling, I love you so much. I would write to you with diamond ink on pages of gold. I would sail the widest ocean to get to you, dear. I'd scale the highest mountain, traverse the burning desert, make any sacrifice just to be near you. That is how much I love you, my darling. P.S. I'll be over tomorrow if it doesn't rain." That is love but with conditions. That is not God's perfect love.

Agape love can only be understood and expressed by someone who knows Jesus Christ. Why? Because agape love is not just love for the saved, it is also love for the sinner. God wants to use us to show love for the unlovable sinner today.

Why did Jesus die? He hung there on the cross, nails in His hands, nails in His feet, blood streaming down His body, transformed by the burden of our sin into something barely recognizable as a human being. God — who created all that was ever created — dying on the cross. Peter denied Him three times. Judas betrayed him for 30 pieces of silver. Barabbas, a rebel murderer, was chosen for freedom by the people instead of Jesus. Why did all these things happen?

The answer, given by Jesus, in John 3:16 says, "For God so loved (agape love) the world, (that is *all* the people of the world) that He gave His only begotten Son, that whosoever believeth in Him should not perish, but have everlasting life. For God sent not His Son into the world to condemn the world; but that the world through Him might be saved."

Jesus Christ is not here on earth physically. Physically, He is at the right hand of God the Father interceding on our behalf. The only physical expression on this earth of God's love, the outward manifestation of His continued perfect love for us, is the church of Jesus Christ. That is why the church is called His Body. When we are saved and become a member of His Body, we become the physical expression of Christ's love on earth. The only way that the unsaved of this world will ever know that God loves them is if somebody puts a face on God and reaches out to them. The following story illustrates what I mean.

The storm was terrible. The wind howled, lightning tore across the sky in jagged bolts, thunder boomed like a raging cannon. A mother thought it would be a perfect opportunity to teach a spiritual lesson to her little daughter, so she said, "Honey, don't be afraid because God is always near." The little girl looked up at her mother and said, "Mama, I know God is always near, but when there's awful lightning and loud thunder like this, I want someone near me who's got skin on!"

Everything and everyone that has life cries out for love — cries out for someone to show them what God is like. I am not sinlessly perfect, but I know I can do one thing, I can love. Because Romans 5:5 says, "The love of God is shed abroad in our hearts by the Holy Ghost which is given to us." He gives us love — but then we must share it with everyone.

Some time ago we began a children's outreach ministry in Lansing. We are reaching out to the children who live in several major housing developments in the area. Our research has shown that no one is working to save these children. Why? Because children don't pay for themselves. It takes money to send the busses, buy the gas, pay for the lights, heat, air conditioning, and for the building in which they will meet. These kids don't have money, so they get overlooked.

When Jesus was hanging on the cross He wasn't worrying about people repaying Him. He made that sacrifice out of love. He loves us all. But how does He express that love today? He is in heaven now. How can we feel that love now? There is only one way. He expresses His love *through* us. When we take care of each other, when we reach out to each other, when we reach down into the gutter and lift up the most unlovable man from the dirt, we are putting "skin" on God!

Chapter Forty

THE LOVE CHAPTER

By Dave Williams

Love is the one thing that Satan can't counterfeit. He can counterfeit gifts of the Spirit, even miracles. He can trick you with all kinds of lies and deception, but he can never counterfeit the love of God because love is something he knows absolutely nothing about.

In First Corinthians, Chapter 13, Paul talks about this kind of agape love. Love wasn't Paul's strong point. He was harsh and judgmental at times. He was especially intolerant of heretics. If I talked in church today the way Paul did back then, many people would be offended — especially if they understood Greek! Yet, God chose Paul to write the Love Chapter.

In the Love Chapter, Paul talks about the Gifts of the Spirit and love. He says we need both. What good is a train without tracks to run on, and what good are tracks if there is no train. If a train is going to be useful, both elements must be present.

"Though I speak with the tongues of men and angels and have not charity (agape love) I am become as sounding brass" (the word brass in the Greek means scrap metal) "or a tinkling cymbal." Without love, all the high sounding phrases and poetry become nothing but noise. "And though I have the gift of prophecy, and understand all mysteries, and all knowledge; and though I have all faith, so that I could remove mountains, and have not charity, it profiteth me nothing." Without love, all the spiritual gifts are just empty exercises. They will not bring help or comfort to anyone.

Even if I give all that I have to the poor, and there is no love in my heart, it will not please God. If you write a check and take it down to the telethon so you can get on TV, that is not love. But if you give what you have to the poor, just to lift them up in love, then you will gain more than you gave. Even if I give my life for the gospel, if there is no love in my heart, it will not please God.

Think of the Asian priests during the Vietnam War. Many sat in the streets of the cities, dumped gasoline on their bodies, and ignited themselves as horrified onlookers watched them burn to death. What did it profit them? In all probability, they're still burning.

Paul goes on to analyze love. He says it is long-suffering, kind, and patient.

A woman came up to me and said, "Brother Dave, I'm going to the lawyer this week; I'm getting rid of my husband. I've put up with him for two months, and that is long enough!" Jesus has been putting up with us for a lot longer than two months. When we demonstrate true love, agape love, we must put up with a lot. Someone told me once that I am very patient with people. How could anyone keep a staff if they demonstrate little or no patience? "Charity suffereth long and is kind; charity envieth not; charity vaunteth not itself, is not puffed up, doth not behave itself unseemly, seeketh not her own, is not easily provoked, thinketh no evil. Rejoiceth not in iniquity, but rejoiceth in the truth" (1 Corinthians 13:4-6).

Sometimes, however, people get the idea that treating others with love means that you become a "Christian doormat" just waiting for the world to walk on you. People fear that expressing Jesus' love to others makes us dopes and weaklings. Jesus could never be described that way! He was fearless in speaking the truth and standing up for what was right. Acting in love doesn't make you a pushover.

Chapter Forty-One
LOVE IS NO PATSY
By Dave Williams

Sometimes we need to speak the truth in love. A grocer in a small town allowed people to buy groceries on credit. People knew he was a Christian and figured they wouldn't have to pay their bills. It got to the point where some of the bills were one or two years behind. People would whine and plead that they didn't have the money to pay this week. He'd forgive them for another week. Yet the people were building new houses and buying new cars; and the grocer was struggling to pay his own bills. One day, while praying, the grocer received an idea. He put a big poster board sign in the window of the grocery store. It said, "I have been unable to pay my bills because several of you have not brought your accounts up to date. Beginning next week, I am going to publish in this window the names of all those who owe me money." Guess what? People came in and said, "I don't want my name in the window. Here's the money I owe you." Love rejoices when the truth wins out. Love doesn't always just lay down and say, "Okay, walk on me, use me and abuse me." Love sometimes has to tell the truth.

Paul continues by talking about love's power, "Beareth all things, believeth all things, hopeth all things, endureth all things. Charity *NEVER* faileth..." (I Corinthians 13:7-8a). There is God's plan for success that is guaranteed never to fail. He said charity will never fail. It doesn't say sometimes it fails, but usually it succeeds. It doesn't say, pay your money and take your chances. No! It says, *"LOVE WILL NEVER FAIL."*

Do you want to run a business? Maybe you're not very good at accounting; maybe you're not even a very good business person — but if you love the people you serve, you will not fail. God says love will never fail; it is durable and eternal. In verse 13 it says, "And now abideth faith, hope, charity, these three; but the greatest of these is charity." Why is love greater than faith? Because faith works by love.

Love is not just feelings or emotions. Love is action. You see, if you're a believer today, the Holy Spirit has already shed this kind of love abroad in your heart. It is in there. Now, it is up to us to share it. In 2 Peter 1:10 it says, "If ye *do* these things...." Do is an active word not a passive one. It means we must put a face on God and become His Body on earth. We must go out and show the world His love. We must act out God's love.

Peter also wrote in 1 Peter 4:8, "*And above all things have fervent charity among yourselves: for charity shall cover the multitude of sins.*" "Above all things" means this should be your priority, your highest focus. This is the crowning component of the high performance life. Covering sins? Many people might think this strange. They will say, "I thought we were to expose one another's sins." The official reason why Richard Dortch was dismissed as an ordained minister was because he failed to reveal the sins of a brother. A Catholic nun said to him, "Reverend Dortch, you sure have a funny religion. In our faith, if a priest revealed the sins of a brother, he would be under discipline. In your religion, if you don't reveal the sins of a brother, you get kicked out."

The Bible says that love will cover a multitude of sins. Charlie was a drunk who lived in Chicago. One day, Charlie stumbled into a church, and the Word of God took root in his life. He accepted Jesus Christ. He said, "Lord, I don't know how I can ever turn away from alcohol, but if you help me, I can turn from it." God delivered him from his drunkenness. The Bible says, "Be not deceived, drunkards shall not inherit the Kingdom of Heaven." God changed Charlie and delivered him. He began to study the Bible, he listened to the pastor week after week, he joined a Sunday School class and began to grow in the faith. He could barely remember what it was like to be free of alcohol, but now he was free at last.

One night, Charlie was walking home from work and came to a drawbridge that was in the up position to allow a boat to go under. Charlie stood and waited for the bridge to come down. But after the boat passed under, the bridge didn't go down. There was some mechanical problem, and the bridge was stuck up. He couldn't get home until it could be fixed. Across the road, Charlie could see the flashing lights of a tavern. The night was dark and cold, and the thought entered Charlie's mind to just go into the tavern for a little while to warm up.

Charlie was sure he would be able to just go in for the warmth, but as soon as he did, all those old feelings and desires came flooding back. He wanted a drink. Just one, he thought. I have been delivered from alcohol; I have freedom in Christ. Just one beer won't hurt me. So he ordered the beer...and another...and another. Much later, Charlie came stumbling out of the bar stone drunk.

Two men from his church happened by at that moment. "Isn't that Charlie?" they said. "Yes, that's Charlie; we've got to help him." They went over to Charlie. Even in his drunken stupor, Charlie was ashamed to be found like that. The two men lifted Charlie up, and putting their arms around him, carried him to their home for the night. As Charlie slept it off, they sat together and prayed for him.

The next morning Charlie felt like he was in hell. He was filled with despair and a sense of utter unworthiness that he had fallen so easily after everything he had learned about sin. But his friends did not rebuke him. They gave him coffee and consolation. They prayed with him, and for him, and said, "Charlie, no one is ever going to know about this but you and us. This will be our secret."

The next week Charlie was back in church. He did not fear the whole church would know of his failure. He was able to put his failure behind him, and today, many years later, he is an ordained minister preaching the gospel of Jesus Christ!

What would have happened if one of those two brothers had felt it was their call to expose Charlie's sin to the entire church? Things might have turned out very differently if Charlie had been made to feel that everyone would be sitting in judgement on him. Proverbs 10:12 says, "Hatred stirs up dissension, but love covers all wrongs." Proverbs 17:9 says, "He who covers an offense promotes love, but whoever repeats the matter separates close friends."

Chapter Forty-Two

EVERYONE NEEDS LOVE

By Dave Williams

Sometimes love can be risky. Jesus said, in Matthew 24, "Because iniquity shall abound, the love of many will wax cold." The reason we don't allow God's love to flow through us to others the way we should is because of sin. Sometimes we need to take a risk and love some people. They may not deserve it, but then neither did you when Jesus died for you. They may not be lovable, but neither were you when God lifted you up.

Every living thing cries out for love, even plants. It has been proven that if you speak to your plants in a loving tone, they will grow better. People need love too. No one is so lost or so hardened that the redeeming love of Jesus Christ can't reach their hearts.

I was going through prayer requests recently. As I read them, I was so grateful to God. There are people out there who have serious problems. It makes me feel good to be able to lift these people and their needs up in prayer. Mary Jo and all our prayer partners pray for these people and their needs. As I got down to the bottom of the stack, I drew out a prayer request that had only three words on it, "I love you." My heart was filled with warm gratitude. I knew those words were meant for me, and I thanked God for the encouragement from this nameless person who took just a moment to write those uplifting words. I took that paper and set it aside, and now, whenever I need a lift, I look at that little slip, and I am reminded of God's love in a very tangible way.

Love can be risky because we have to rescue people that are in situations where we don't want to go to help them. In a book by James Moore, there is a story about Lawi, a little African boy. He lived in a grass hut with his family. One day his parents were going out to the fields, and they put Lawi in charge of babysitting his little brother. While his little brother slept, Lawi worked outside. Suddenly, the hut caught on fire. Lawi saw people standing around the hut while inside his baby brother screamed for help, but nobody dared to go into the hut to rescue him.

Lawi ran as fast as he could and dashed into the blazing hut. Flames were leaping everywhere; some burning debris blocked him from his little brother. He pushed it aside with his hands and snatched his brother up. Risking his life, he saved his brother from the smoke and flames.

The headman of the village said, "Lawi, you were very brave. What were you thinking when you ran into the burning hut?"

"I wasn't thinking about anything," Lawi responded. "I just heard my brother crying."

All around us there are people dangling over the flames of hell. Hell is a real place, and people are in real danger of ending up there. They are crying out for salvation, and the only solution is to believe in Jesus Christ and trust in Him as their Savior. Their only hope is for the saved of the world, you and I, to reach out to them in love and offer them this precious gift. The love we need to give is not eros (erotic love), or even philos (brotherly love), but agape love, God's perfect love for us all. It is the love with no strings or conditions attached. It is the love for the unlovable and undeserving. That is how God loves you and me.

We cannot put this love in our hearts. Only the Holy Spirit can do that. But we can act on that love by faith. When we do, we will see the world come to Jesus Christ in a great wave of revival. I believe that!

Proverbs 21:21 says, "He who pursues righteousness and love, finds three things: life, prosperity, and honor." If you want to be the kind of person who can say with assurance, "I am really living," then be a person who demonstrates love. Do you want prosperity? Prosperity is the natural, inevitable result of loving generosity. Do you want honor? Be the kind of person who loves, and honor will find you; you won't need to seek it. Be an expression of God's love on earth, and all your dreams will come true.

Chapter Forty-Three
WINNER OR LOSER? YOUR CHOICE!
By Dave Williams

When you look at your own life, what do you see? Do you see a life that reflects the fulfillment of God's will for you? Are you experiencing victory racing tirelessly in the fast lane of high performance achievement? Or, are you plagued by failure and defeat? Do you feel like a victim of life's troubles — or a conqueror in the Lord Jesus Christ?

Yielding to the Holy Spirit and developing the qualities of a high performance winner will produce terrific benefits in your life. You will thrive, achieve, and succeed with a heart filled with the joy of loving the Lord and serving Him. Your life will be exciting and vital, never humdrum.

The difference between victory and defeat, success and failure, is directly proportional to your willingness to grow in your Christian faith. You must be willing to take responsibility and grow. You must see the power of adding the nine qualities of a high performance believer into your life.

Remember, the stakes are high. The lost of the world are waiting for someone just like you to reach them. If you are struggling, barely moving forward, what will you have to offer those who need to hear the good news of Jesus Christ? When you enter heaven, will you receive the victor's welcome? Will you hear those words every Christian dreams of hearing, "Well done, good and faithful servant!" from the lips of Jesus?

Put these additives into your spiritual engine, and you will find yourself drawing ever closer to our Lord Jesus Christ, and your Christian walk will be forever changed for the better.

The choice is yours. Choose the right spiritual additives for high performance living, and you will find yourself racing in the fast lane, not running on empty.

> *But they that wait upon the Lord*
> *shall renew their strength; they shall*
> *mount up with wings as eagles; they*
> *shall run, and not be weary; and they*
> *shall walk, and not faint.*
>
> Isaiah 40:31

About the Authors

Dick Mills has spent a lifetime as a soldier in the Army of the Lord. Since surrendering his life in 1943, and saying an eternal "yes" to God to do His will, his ministry has been characterized by unique gifts and great success.

In 1966, he became a part of the then-emerging Charismatic Renewal. Transcending denominational barriers, his ministry led him to speak at thousands of churches all over the world. He still maintains a busy schedule as an evangelist. Dick has many ministry opportunities in radio, television, books, tapes, and videos. He is the author of *He Spoke and I was Strengthened*, with over 150,000 copies now in print. He is also a popular speaker at college and university campus meetings as well as home groups. Years of Bible study have made Dick one of the foremost authorities on Bible scholarship. Most recently, Dick and his son David wrote the "World Wealth" section to the *Spirit Filled Life Bible*, which was released in 1991.

The Holy Spirit moves through Dick Mills to teach, edify, and uplift. His ministry is to the congregation, as well as the individual, as the Lord speaks through him with personal words of wisdom, encouragement, and prophecy. His mission is to inform, enlighten, and motivate people to a higher level of commitment to God.

Dave Williams is Pastor of Mount Hope Church and International Outreach Ministries in Lansing, Michigan.

Dave's ministry is characterized by a dynamic and inspirational teaching style. He is a popular speaker in the United States and many foreign countries, including South Africa, and England. He is the author of *The New Life... The Start of Something Wonderful*, an international best seller now in its twelfth printing. He has authored over 30 other books, appears regularly on radio and TV, and his leadership training course, *The School of Pacesetting Leadership*, is popular not only in churches, but in the business world as well.

His mission is threefold: To lead people into a deep, fruitful relationship with the Lord Jesus Christ, to inspire people to walk in God's perfect will, and to motivate believers to reach their greatest potential for God.